WHITE-TAILED DEER

THE HUNTING & FISHING LIBRARY®

By Gary Clancy and Larry R. Nelson

GARY CLANCY, one of the country's top deer-hunting authorities, has hunted whitetails in a dozen states using rifles, shotguns, muzzleloaders and bows. His writings have been published in many national and regional outdoor magazines.

LARRY R. NELSON has been a professional wildlife manager for 23 years, with extensive experience in farmland deer management. He's hunted whitetails since childhood with rifles, shotguns and muzzleloaders.

JAY McANINCH is a professional deer researcher with 15 years of experience in the north central and northeastern states. He is a lecturer and consultant on whitetail issues, and an avid bowhunter.

CY DECOSSE INCORPORATED
Chairman: Cy DeCosse
President: James B. Maus
Executive Vice President: William B. Jones

WHITE-TAILED DEER
Project Director: Dick Sternberg
Authors: Gary Clancy, Larry R. Nelson
Editors: Dick Sternberg, Tom Carpenter
Technical Advisor and Editor: Jay McAninch
Project Managers: Joseph Cella, Tracy Wright
Senior Art Director: Bradley Springer
Principal Photographer: Mike Hehner
Photo Director: Eric Lindberg
Photo Assistants: Steve Hauge, Jim Moynagh
Research Director: Eric Lindberg
Researchers: Steve Hauge, Mike Hehner, Jim Moynagh
Director of Development, Planning & Production: Jim Bindas
Production Manager: Amelia Merz
Electronic Publishing Analyst: Kevin D. Frakes
Typesetting: Linda Schloegel
Production Staff: Janice Cauley, Joe Fahey, Peter Gloege, Mark Jacobson, Duane John, Dave Schelitzche, Nik Wogstad
Photo Studio Supervisor: Rebecca Boyle
Staff Photographers: Rex Irmen, John Lauenstein, Bill Lindner, Mark Macemon, Mette Nielsen, Mike Parker, Cathleen Shannon
Shop Supervisor: Greg Wallace
Prop Stylist: Jim Huntley
Illustrators: Thomas Boll, Mary Albury-Noyes, Bradley Springer

Main Contributing Photographers: Daniel J. Cox, Denver Bryan/Images on the Wildside, Mike Biggs
Contributing Photographers: Adirondack Museum; Erwin Bauer/Wildstock; Boone and Crockett Club; Dana C. Bryan/Florida Park Service; Soc Clay; Michael Collier; Jeanne Drake; Tom Edwards; Tim Flanigan/Pennsylvania Game Commission; Michael H. Francis; Eric Lindberg; Maine Fish and Game Department; Bill Marchel; Keith McCaffery/Wisconsin Department of Natural Resources; David Milburn/Lightworks, Inc.; Minnesota Department of Natural Resources; Nebraska Game and Parks Commission; Larry R. Nelson/Minnesota Department of Natural Resources; Jim Rathert/Missouri Department of Conservation; Lynn L. Rogers; Leonard Lee Rue III; University of Minnesota; Bill Vaznis; Jan Wassink

Cooperating Individuals and Agencies: Ammocraft – Don Parsons; Arkansas Game and Fish Commission – Nick Smith; Bald Eagle Sports – Jim Kohler; Alfred Berner; Binocular City, Inc. – William Neish; Edward Boggess; Boone and Crockett Club; Larry Boughten; Buckhorn Hunting Club – Bob Doolittle; Burger Brothers – John Goplin, Tom Zrust; Bwana Archery – John and Sharon Larson; Carlos Avery Wildlife Management Area – Peggy Calahant, Roger Johnson, Lloyd Knudson; Cedar Ridge Hunting Club – Howard Miller, Alvin Sharp; James Deaner; Deer and Deer Hunting Magazine – Robert Wegner; Joe Drake; Dr. Andrew E. Edin; Rory Gunderson; Mike Hamm; Anthony J. Hansen; Iowa Conservation Commission – Lee Gladfelter; Thomas Isley; Ron Jackson; Chris Johnson; Les Johnson; Al Marion; Michigan Department of Natural Resources – John Ozaga; Greg Miller; Minnesota Department of Natural Resources – George Meadows, Larry Milbridge; Mississippi Department of Economic Development – John Horhn; Mississippi Department of Wildlife Conservation – Bill Lunceford; Missouri Department of Conservation – Dr. Lonnie Hansen, Ollie Torgerson; Moon Valley Shooting

Range – Scott Blosberg, Wally Griepentrog; North American Taxidermy – Tom Witbeck; Pat Olson; Outdoorsman Gun Shop; Keith Partridge; John Phillips; Pope and Young Club – Glen Hisey; Sierra, The Bulletsmiths – David Brown; Marty Stubstad; Larry Swenson; J. L. Trabue Company, Inc. – Frank Harriman; United States Department of Agriculture – Rick Owens; University of Georgia – Dr. Victor Nettles; University of Minnesota – Dr. Peter Jordan; Warner Nature Center – Charlie Johnston; Larry Weishuhn; John Weiss; West Virginia Department of Natural Resources – Gordon Robertson; West Virginia University – Dr. Dave Samuel; Minnesota Deer Classic – Hugh Price; Wisconsin Department of Natural Resources – Keith McCaffery; Jack Wood

Cooperating Manufacturers: Accra; The Allen Company, Inc. – Beverly Meyers; ATSKO/Sno Seal Company – Kurt von Besser; Browning – Paul Thompson; Burris Company, Inc. – Gordon McClain; Bushnell – Richard Babcock, Barbara Mellum, Don Robertson; Cabela's, Inc. – Tony Dolle, Dennis Highby; Darton Archery – Tom Rogers; Easton Aluminum, Inc. – Jim Easton, Cathy Velardi; Eddie Salter Calls; Federal Cartridge Company – Mike Larson, Bill Stevens; Forrester Outdoor Products – Joe Forrester; Hoyt USA – Bill Krenz; Lohman Mfg. Company, Inc. – Brad Harris; Lone Wolf, Inc. – Andrae and Nick D'Acquisto; Modern Muzzleloading, Inc. – William Knight; Mountain State Muzzleloading Supplies, Inc.; Nikon, Inc. – Howard Hyman; Olin-Winchester – John R. Falk; Realtree Products, Inc. – Bill Jordan; Remington Arms Company – Dick Dietz; Sturm, Ruger & Company, Inc.; Trebark Camouflage – Jim Crumley; True Shot Enterprises – Sonny Jones; Warren & Sweat Mfg. Company, Inc. – Ray McIntyre

Color Separations: Scantrans Pte. Ltd.
Printing: R. R. Donnelley & Sons, Co. (1291)

Library of Congress
Cataloging-in-Publication Data

Clancy, Gary.
White-tailed deer / Gary Clancy & Larry R. Nelson.
p. cm. – (The Hunting & fishing library)
Includes index.
ISBN 0-86573-036-9
1. White-tailed deer hunting. 2. White-tailed deer. I. Nelson, Larry R. II. Title. III. Series.
SK301.C52 1991   91-16959
799.2'77357 – dc20

2

Contents

Introduction

No other big-game animal has captured the hearts and imaginations of hunters like the white-tailed deer. From the Texas scrub to the moss-draped thickets of Mississippi to fertile midwestern farmlands or the pine forests of Maine, the whitetail is America's most popular big-game animal.

And for good reason. More than 20 million whitetails now inhabit the United States and Canada, compared to only a few hundred thousand in the early 1900s. The majority of the country's hunters have a good chance of bagging a deer within a short drive of their home.

Whether you hunt them for food, for a trophy rack or for the fond memories of time spent at the deer shack, whitetails are challenging opponents. Unless you understand how they behave, and use the best hunting technique for the conditions, their superb senses of smell and hearing give them the edge.

White-tailed Deer will acquaint you with all aspects of whitetail behavior. You'll learn what habitats they prefer; how they react to changes in weather; when, where and how they feed; how they use their senses; and how they communicate with each other. Also included is a detailed account of each stage in the breeding cycle – information of vital importance in planning your hunting strategy.

No matter whether you hunt with a rifle, shotgun, bow and arrow, muzzleloader or pistol, this book will show you exactly what equipment, accessories and clothing to buy. You'll also learn how to interpret ballistics and arrow selection tables.

How you prepare for the hunt is just as important as how you operate in the field. We'll provide some valuable tips on finding good places to hunt, preseason scouting, sighting in firearms and bows, marksmanship and maximizing your chances of a clean kill by proper shot placement. A concise section on hunting safety is required reading.

Many longtime deer hunters become set in their ways; some always stand-hunt, some routinely still-

hunt and others prefer to drive, often in the same location year after year. But such rigidity seldom leads to consistent success. This book details the best techniques for the terrain, stage of the season, time of day and weather conditions. Step-by-step color photos and diagrams describe every important whitetail hunting strategy. Also included are dozens of tips experts use to gain that critical edge.

Should you wound a deer, it's your responsibility to do everything possible to find it. But successful tracking requires special skills. You'll learn how to interpret different types of blood sign and how to proceed based on what you see.

Many people prefer venison to beef, and nutrition authorities say it's much healthier. But you must field-dress the animal properly to get quality meat. We've included a 12-step photo sequence that guides you through the field-dressing process. Should you shoot "one for the wall," we'll show you how to cape it out so your taxidermist can deliver a perfect trophy.

This book always goes well beyond the basics, revealing many innovative techniques that experienced

hunters use in specific situations. We detail the best strategies for hunting on opening day, in suburban areas, in wetlands and in standing corn. You'll discover how to rattle in a buck, and how to properly use scents to improve your odds. Finally, you'll get some expert advice on bagging a trophy buck.

With more than 12 million deer hunters in the United States alone, there's no shortage of books on the subject. Unfortunately, some new books contain "breakthrough" information and "medicine-show" tactics that go far beyond existing biological fact.

Although this type of material has strong market appeal, it is misleading and in most cases counterproductive to hunting success.

Written by established hunting authorities with input from many of the country's leading whitetail biologists, *White-tailed Deer* contains a wealth of state-of-the-art, biologically sound information. Whether you're a first-time deer hunter or a trophy-buck addict, you can boost your odds by studying this book and putting its advice to work as you plan future whitetail hunts.

Understanding
White-tailed Deer

Whitetail Basics

The beauty and grace of the elusive whitetail fascinates hunters and nonhunters alike. This cunning deer has long been our country's most popular and numerous big-game animal.

Named for its most prominent feature, the whitetail holds its tail upright when alarmed, exposing a snowy white underside and white rump patch that strike a warning to other deer.

White patches around the muzzle, throat, eyes, ears and belly are smaller and less noticeable. On rare occasion, you'll see albino (all white with pink eyes) or melanistic (dark phase) deer, or even *piebald* deer, with scattered white blotches.

The rest of an adult's summer coat is reddish brown. By late summer, however, they shed their summer coat and grow a thick, brownish-gray winter coat.

Relatively dark winter coats on northern deer absorb sunlight, helping to keep the animal warm. Whitetails in the Southwest's warm, open brushlands have lighter-colored summer coats, which reflect sunlight.

A whitetail's winter coat is several times thicker than the summer coat. It has a dense layer of short, white underfur and hollow guard hairs, which combine to give the coat excellent insulating properties. The coat is also water-repellent, so precipitation does not penetrate to the skin.

The thin summer coat has a reddish hue (photo above)

← *The gray winter coat is many times thicker*

Whitetail fawns are usually born in May or June. They weigh 4 to 8 pounds at birth. Their reddish coat is covered with white spots, which serve as camouflage. The spots disappear when they develop their winter coat, but a rare late-born fawn still has spots or reddish hair after the season begins.

Fawns from good habitat weigh 80 to 100 pounds by fall

Even large whitetails are deceptively short. Adults measure only 30 to 40 inches tall at the shoulder. They typically measure 5 to 6 feet from nose to tail, but may reach 8 feet.

Bucks usually outweigh does of the same age by at least 25 percent. Northern deer tend to be larger and heavier than southern deer. For example, the largest whitetail on record was a Minnesota buck with a live weight estimated at 511 pounds. On the other hand, adult bucks in the Florida Keys weigh as little as 50 pounds. In various regions of the United States, bucks average from 100 to 150 pounds. Deer over 300 pounds are exceptional anywhere.

The whitetail's sophisticated 4-part stomach (p. 19) digests everything from cactus to acorns and produces heat as a by-product. Because they can eat so many different foods, they can live in a wide variety of habitats.

Whitetails have black cloven hooves, and dewclaws. Yearling and adult bucks grow antlers, and in extremely rare cases, does grow them too.

Deer possess four external sets of scent glands. During the breeding season, bucks mark rubs (p. 29) and branches overhanging scrapes

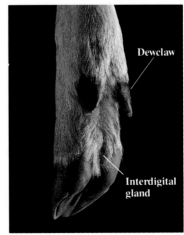

Deer hoof, showing dewclaw and position of interdigital gland

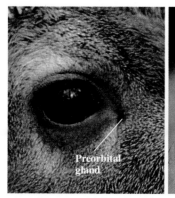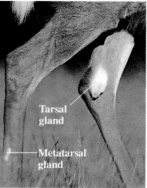

Preorbital glands (left) are at the lower front corner of the eye; tarsal and metatarsal glands (right) are on the back legs

(p. 30) with scent from the preorbital glands. Bucks also mark scrapes by urinating on their spongelike tarsal glands while rubbing them together and squeezing out old, strong-smelling urine (p. 31). The metatarsal and interdigital glands have sometimes been credited for scenting scrapes and tracks. However, the true role of these glands has never been conclusively proven.

Long, slender legs and strong upper leg muscles give whitetails agility and allow them to run up to 40 miles per hour for short distances and leap 8 feet high with a running jump. They trot and gallop gracefully, and can easily swim several miles.

Range of North American Deer Species

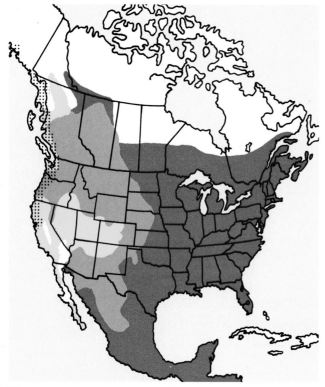

■ White-tailed deer   □ Mule deer
■ White-tailed and mule deer combined
▦ Black-tailed deer

How to Identify Whitetails

ANTLERS AND EARS. Points, normally unbranched, arise from continuous main beams that curve forward and inward. The ears are about half the length of the muzzle.

How to Identify Mule Deer and Black-tailed Deer

ANTLERS AND EARS. Main antler beams divide about an ear length from the head, with each end branching again. The ears are about ¾ the length of the muzzle.

TAIL. The outside of a lowered tail is the same color as the deer's back; the edges and underside are white.

GAIT. Whitetails bound with long, graceful strides mixed with high leaps. They also trot with their head erect and pointed forward. Whether trotting or bounding, they hold their tail up.

TAIL. On mule deer (top), the tail is white with a black tip; on blacktails (bottom), all black on the outside.

GAIT. Stotting, or stiff-legged bounding in jackrabbit style, characterizes mule and black-tailed deer. All four feet touch the ground simultaneously with each bound. Both species run with the tail down.

Weather

Veteran hunters know that weather has a dramatic effect on whitetails, and they plan their hunting strategy accordingly.

Temperature has a strong influence on deer movement. On warm summer days, whitetails feed during the first hour of daylight, and again after sundown and into the night. They spend most of the day in cool, shady spots such as dense hardwood and conifer stands, woodlots, wooded stream corridors, shrub thickets and wetlands with tall vegetation.

When the temperature rises above freezing in winter, deer behave much the same as on a warm day

Deer are usually active in light rain but will search out dense cover in heavy rain

Whitetails bed down in snowy weather

in summer. They're actually too warm because of their heavy winter coat. At colder temperatures, down to 0°F, whitetails spend most of their day in sunny areas sheltered from the wind. They feed between mid-morning and mid-afternoon. At temperatures below zero, deer lose heat more rapidly, so they must eat more food. Their feeding periods are longer, sometimes all day and all night in the coldest weather. The extra movement associated with feeding also helps keep them warm.

Extreme weather conditions may cause whitetails to alter their normal behavior patterns. In northern forests, when faced with a prolonged period of deep snow, they often congregate in sheltered areas called *deer yards*. A good yard helps protect them from the elements and provides quality winter foods. Even though their metabolic rate decreases, they may run out of food and starve to death if deep snow keeps them yarded up too long.

In the plains and deserts of the South and West, drought conditions may force whitetails into dense, brushy areas that provide shade and moist food, or to watering areas such as streams, irrigation ditches and water holes. In coastal plains, whitetails congregate in bottomland hardwoods when rainy weather results in high water.

Wind velocity also impacts deer activity. Deer move about most when the wind is less than 10 mph. In blustery winds, deer cannot smell or hear well

enough to detect danger; they remain in a state of high alert, even when bedded.

During windy weather, deer spend their time in sheltered areas such as cattail swamps, wooded gullies or thick pine plantations. In some cases, they move to areas where they can see long distances.

In light rain, snow or sleet, deer remain active, often feeding in open areas. But heavy precipitation keeps them in dense cover, frequently in thick conifers or other trees where the canopy offers some protection.

Whitetails have an uncanny ability to sense impending weather changes. In the hours before a severe storm, they may feed and move about even if the weather is warm. They stay in heavy cover during the storm, but as soon as it subsides, they start to move again. After a heavy snowstorm, however, deer may stay in cover for two or three days.

Always take the weather into account when considering what hunting technique to use. For instance, during a light drizzle, you'd be better off still-hunting than stand-hunting. High winds also limit the effectiveness of rattling and calling, because the sound doesn't carry well.

If you expect the day to be warm and calm, try stand-hunting in the cooler morning and evening hours, when deer will most likely be on the move. During midday, when the woods are quiet, organize a drive or try float-hunting.

DEER YARDS vary from white-cedar swamps in northern forests to cornfields in agricultural areas. In a severe winter, hundreds of deer may congregate in a single yard. A typical yarding area draws whitetails from 5 to 10 miles away.

13

Whitetails thrive where there's plenty of edge cover

Whitetail Habitat

Whitetails can adapt to a broad spectrum of conditions, ranging from scorching tropical heat to bitter cold and belly-deep snow.

But no matter where deer live, the habitat must furnish adequate food, water and cover. An individual deer establishes a *home range*, a plot of ground that supplies all these basic needs. Throughout its lifetime, the animal will rarely leave this familiar turf.

HABITAT REQUIREMENTS. Whitetails require an abundant food supply (p. 18) consisting mainly of grasses and *forbs*, low-growing, broad-leaved plants. In winter, when green plants are not available, deer eat crops and crop residues, nuts and *browse*, meaning buds and attached twigs.

Whitetails can survive for long periods without drinking, if their food has a high water content. The less water available in the food, the more they must get from streams, lakes, potholes or other surface-water sources. Lack of water may limit deer populations in arid regions. In the North, deer get their wintertime water by eating snow.

Deer need heavy cover, not only to elude hunters, but to protect them from the elements. Where dense

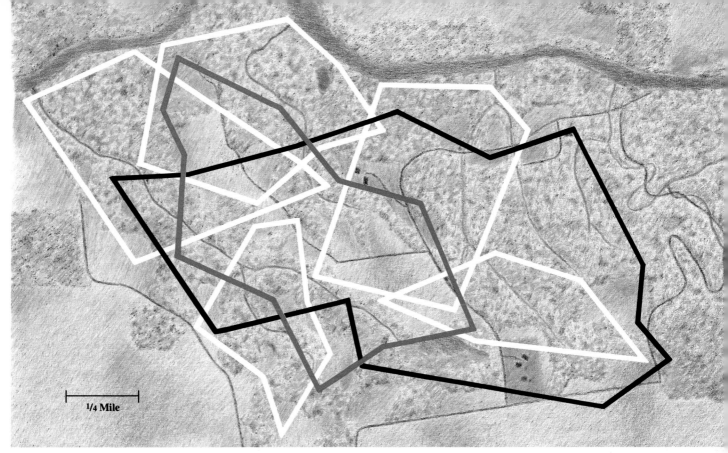

HOME RANGE of Iowa whitetails was studied using radio telemetry. The study area, typical mixed forest and agricultural land, contained the home ranges of 5 adult does (white lines), 1 adult buck (red line) and 1 yearling buck (black line). The adult buck's home range was larger than that of any doe, and it overlapped the range of each doe. The yearling buck's home range also overlapped the range of each doe, but was much larger than that of the adult buck, mainly because the older buck drove the yearling away from the prime breeding area.

1/4 Mile

cover is lacking, rugged terrain, such as a gully cutting through an open prairie, provides shelter and escape cover.

Whitetails are creatures of the *edge* – the zone between two different types of habitat, such as a forest and a field. An edge affords easy access to cover plus a variety of foods, from grasses and forbs to nuts and browse. Patchworks, rather than vast expanses of a single type of cover, support the densest deer populations because they have more edge habitat.

Succession gradually changes deer habitat. For example, a young forest is excellent for whitetails because it has plenty of edge, abundant food and good escape cover. But as the forest matures, edge disappears as a thick canopy develops. The forest floor becomes shaded, eliminating the plants that provide food and cover.

HOME RANGE. By becoming intimately familiar with a certain area, a deer can react instinctively when danger threatens. In unfamiliar territory, a deer has no knowledge of escape routes and hiding spots, so it's more likely to commit a fatal mistake.

Most bucks spend their lives in home ranges of 500 to 1,000 acres; does, 300 to 600 acres. Home ranges of bucks and does are larger in open habitats or unbroken forest.

Buck home ranges on the Texas plains, for instance, cover up to 5,000 acres; in mixed fields and forests of Wisconsin, only 200 acres.

Adult bucks and does usually stay on the same home ranges from one year to the next, except yearling bucks often move to new ones. Extreme harassment, such as pursuit by dogs, may temporarily drive them off, but they usually return within hours. In a Georgia study, heavy hunting pressure (64 hunters per square mile) temporarily pushed deer out of their home ranges. But it is virtually impossible for a small group of hunters to force the deer out.

Normally, a spooked whitetail doesn't go far. A deer with a 200-acre home range, for instance, can run only a few hundred yards before crossing into unfamiliar territory. Whitetails spooked by humans generally run less than 100 yards, then slip into familiar escape cover.

Many think deer avoid hunters by circling downwind to watch what's trailing them. But the deer is simply doubling back to stay on its home range while making its escape.

HABITAT TYPES. Following are the most common types of whitetail habitat:

Agricultural and Prairie – Most of this flat or gently rolling terrain is intensively farmed or grazed. Woody cover is limited to stream corridors and small woodlots, but deer often use crops as cover. Cold, snowy winters may limit food availability. Human populations are moderate, but hunting seasons efficiently control deer numbers.

Northern Forests – This densely wooded terrain ranges from flat to hilly. Logging is common and the human population low. Because of the vast amount of deer cover, the impact of hunting is comparatively light. Food production is limited where the forest is continuous with no clearings; cold weather and deep snow limit food availability and deer movements in winter.

Central and Eastern Forests – This patchwork of fields and forests lies on rolling to low-mountain topography. The human population is high and hunting pressure heavy. Forest industries and small farms with livestock dominate land use. Moderate temperatures and snowfall in winter mean that deer normally have adequate food.

Coastal Plain – This habitat has a mix of wetlands, forests and agricultural land, mainly cropland and pasture. Despite the high human population, hunting seasons often don't control deer populations, so there may be food shortages. Winters are mild and have little effect on deer populations.

Western Plains – The flat to gently rolling terrain is grazed or intensively farmed, sometimes with irrigation. Although cover is limited, deer spend their time along wooded streams and in small woodlots, tall grasslands and standing crops. Hunters do well because the limited cover concentrates deer. Severe winter cold and snow may limit deer survival in the northern reaches of the plains.

Common Whitetail Habitats

AGRICULTURAL AND PRAIRIE habitat consists of cropland, primarily corn, soybeans, oats and alfalfa, along with pasture and native grassland. Oak, maple, elm, ash, box elder and basswood grow along streams and in woodlots.

CENTRAL AND EASTERN FORESTS are dominated by stands of oak and hickory and sometimes shortleaf pine. Cropfields, pastures and prairie remnants break up the forest and provide edge habitat.

Other Important Whitetail Habitats

WESTERN FORESTS AND MOUNTAINS, particularly the foothills, hold some deer. Trees and shrubs include aspen, spruce, fir, scrub oak, mahogany and sagebrush.

16

NORTHERN FORESTS often contain mixed stands of maple, beech, birch, ash, aspen, hickory, basswood, oak, spruce, fir, pine, hemlock and cedar. The most productive forests are broken by openings such as power-line corridors, roads and wetlands. Some forests are virtually roadless, however, and considered wilderness.

COASTAL PLAINS habitat is largely marsh with some cropland. Trees include pine, oak, hickory, sweetbay, redbay, maple, willow, cottonwood, sycamore, elm and ash.

WESTERN PLAINS are mostly grasslands, with fields of wheat, corn, milo, oats and alfalfa, often irrigated. Cottonwood, plum, sumac, oak and sagebrush line the streambanks.

FOOTHILLS in deserts of New Mexico and Arizona support the Coues deer, usually at elevations of 4,000 to 8,000 feet, where oaks and pines line intermittent streams.

THE FLORIDA KEYS are home to the tiny Key deer, an endangered species. Mangrove, palmetto, Indian mulberry, white-indigo berry and palm trees are dominant plants.

Food, Feeding & Digestion

Like cattle, whitetails are ruminants, or "cud chewers." They gulp food without chewing and store it in the *rumen*, the first and largest chamber of their 4-part stomach. This feeding behavior is advantageous in severe weather or when hunting pressure is heavy. The deer can feed rapidly when the opportunity presents itself, easily consuming five pounds of food in a half-hour. Then they retreat to the safety of heavy cover.

Once bedded, the deer regurgitates food from its rumen, chews its cud (the term for regurgitated food) and swallows it. The food then passes through the other stomach chambers for further digestion (opposite page).

The rumination process allows whitetails to digest a wide variety of plant material. Primarily grazers, deer gain weight quickly during the growing season by consuming grasses, forbs, legumes, agricultural crops (especially corn and soybeans), flowers, nuts, fruits, vegetables, emergent aquatics, mushrooms, winter buds of woody plants and high-moisture succulents such as cactus.

Heat produced by the digestive process affects deer behavior. Hot weather, along with the heat of digestion, reduces their activity; they seek cover in a cool, shady spot. On winter nights, the rumen acts like a furnace. Except in the coldest weather, deer can stay bedded without losing so much heat that they have to get up and move around.

Digestion is very efficient; only about 5 percent of the food cannot be digested and is expelled as hard, relatively dry pellets.

Deer have no upper front teeth. To eat a bud, for instance, they pinch it between their lower front teeth and

Whitetail chewing cud

THE STOMACH consists of four chambers. The largest is (1) the rumen which stores food until it is regurgitated and rechewed. Reswallowed food ferments in the rumen and the second chamber, (2) the reticulum. Then it passes to the (3) omasum and (4) abomasum, which absorb water and minerals and break down proteins.

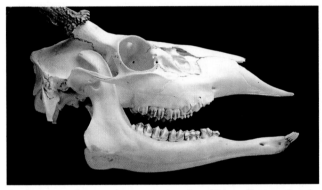

Lack of upper front teeth prevents deer from biting off stems cleanly

the "tire tread" roof of their mouth, then pull. Frayed twig ends are a sure sign of deer feeding activity.

Bucks feed heavily and build up fat reserves in spring and summer. But during the breeding season, adult bucks eat very little and use up fat as they pursue does and spar with other bucks. Although does consume large quantities of food in summer, they lose weight while nursing their fawns. They regain weight rapidly in fall in preparation for pregnancy.

Whitetails may have a tough time finding nourishing food in winter. Snow covers high-quality foods such as acorns and crop residue, forcing deer to eat browse. Their activity and metabolism slow down, and they typically lose 20 percent of their weight as they use up fat reserves. Severe cold and deep snow aggravate the problem even more because they increase the energy drain.

Severe droughts and floods can also cause food shortages. Conservation agencies monitor the condition of deer herds, and if these conditions persist too long, may call upon sportsmen's groups to cooperate in distributing high-quality deer foods such as alfalfa pellets. Although feeding programs are expensive and deer in remote habitats, such as northern forests, are difficult to reach, they can be saved if feeding starts early enough. In a severe winter, however, deer may not have time to develop the rumen bacteria that will digest the new food, so they could starve to death with a full stomach. Any deer that loses more than 40 percent of its body weight will not recover.

How much water deer require depends on the climate, time of year, their activity level and the moisture content of their food. Given a choice, deer

Water holes supplement water from food

eat the food with the highest moisture level. In wet climates, deer get practically all of their water from their food. In dry climates, they require additional water and may visit water holes several times a day. In winter, they get additional water by eating snow.

NON-TYPICAL RACKS have many abnormal tines branching from regular tines, or growing sideways or down. This 44-pointer, the current Boone and Crockett record, has main beams measuring 24⅛ and 23⅜ inches. The greatest spread (across main beams or points) is 33⅜ inches. The rack scored 337⅞ points.

Age, Growth & Antler Development

How long deer live, how large they grow and the size of their antlers are popular but often misunderstood topics. The following discussion reflects the latest research on these subjects.

AGE. Despite many "deer-camp" stories to the contrary, whitetail bucks seldom live longer than 2 or 3 years in areas that are hunted. The oldest wild buck on record is a 10-year-old from an unhunted region of Ohio.

Normally, does live more than twice as long as bucks. The oldest wild whitetail on record is a 22-year-old doe from New Jersey.

To set hunting regulations, biologists must determine the age composition of the herd. The most reliable but time-consuming technique for determining a deer's age involves slicing a front tooth, staining the cross section, and counting the annual growth rings. More commonly biologists examine the pattern of tooth replacement and wear to quickly distinguish between fawns, yearlings and adults (opposite page).

Antler size and the number of points are generally poor indicators of age because many variables affect antler growth.

GROWTH. Nutrition, sex, age, latitude and genetics determine a deer's growth rate and ultimate size.

Although deer grow to almost full length and height as yearlings, they gain in bulk for a few years thereafter. A yearling buck in the eastern forest, for example, may measure 30 inches at the shoulder, 65 inches from nose to tail and weigh 130 pounds at the

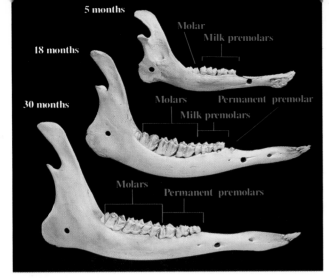

ESTIMATE a deer's age from its teeth. A fawn (top) has 3 milk premolars and 1 molar. A yearling (middle), has 3 molars. The first permanent premolar has pushed out the milk premolar. The other milk premolars will also be replaced, the third one (a tricuspid) by a bicuspid. On an adult (bottom), the molars are worn more than a yearling's.

Average Weight of 1½-Year-Old Bucks (forested habitat)

LOCATION & LATITUDE		WEIGHT
New York	43-45 ° N	135 lbs.
Ohio	40-41 ° N	114 lbs.
Missouri	37-38 ° N	96 lbs.
Arkansas	34-36 ° N	88 lbs.
Texas	30-32 ° N	70 lbs.

TYPICAL RACKS are fairly symmetrical, although they may have a different number of tines on each side. This 13-pointer, the current Montana record, has main beams 27⅜ and 27½ inches long. The greatest spread is 24⅜ inches. The rack scored 199⅜ points.

start of the breeding season; at 2½ years old, this deer measures 34 inches at the shoulder, 75 inches in length and weighs 180 pounds.

Farmland deer grow faster than their forest counterparts, mainly because of better nutrition. A yearling buck may weigh close to 200 pounds; a 2½-year-old buck, 250 pounds.

The average 2½-year-old adult buck is about 20 percent taller and longer than a doe of the same age, and outweighs her by about 30 percent. However, weight differences vary greatly in different habitat types and in different years, so it's not unusual for bucks to weigh twice as much as does of the same age.

Like most mammals, whitetails in the northern part of their range grow larger than those in the southern part (see above chart). A larger body has less surface area in comparison to its bulk. This reduces the rate of heat loss, an advantage during long, cold winters.

Even in the same habitat type, some deer grow larger than others because of genetic differences.

ANTLER DEVELOPMENT. Antlers are projections of true bone that grow from *pedicles*, small stalk-like structures above and in front of a buck's ears. Bucks shed their antlers after the breeding season and grow new, usually larger, ones the following year.

Some hunters refer to antlers as horns, but horns are continuously growing, modified hair sheaths that cover a permanent bony projection. Cows, buffalo, pronghorns, goats and members of the sheep family have horns, not antlers.

Big whitetails can have small antlers and small whitetails can have big antlers. Just as genetics, age and nutrition determine body size, they also determine antler size and shape. Injuries also affect antler development. In rare instances, a hormonal imbalance causes a doe to grow antlers.

Genetics set the limits for antler size and form, allowing some bucks to grow large antlers and limiting antler size on others. Dominant bucks are usually large and have thick antlers with lots of points. They tend to produce offspring that also have large bodies and antlers. Genetics and accidents also control whether racks will be typical or non-typical. Unusual antler characteristics, such as drop points, a wide spread or long tines, are often carried through several generations of bucks.

Male fawns (left) have pedicles; female fawns (right) do not

As bucks age, they usually grow larger, thicker antlers. Fawn males, called "button bucks," have pedicles but no antlers. A yearling's antlers can range from spikes to six-pointers or better but are only about half the thickness they can be when the deer reaches maturity. Deer in good condition usually grow their largest antlers between ages 3 and 7, if they live that long.

Nutrition is the major factor regulating antler size. Poor nutrition caused by overpopulation, severe weather or inferior habitat is a problem in many areas. A farmland yearling can grow a bigger rack than a 3-year-old in a mature forest because it has access to more and higher-quality food. Adult bucks in poor condition may never grow big racks, despite proper genetics. On the other hand, a buck in good physical condition still needs the right genetic code to grow record-book antlers.

The ratio of daylight to darkness, or *photoperiod*, controls antler cycles throughout most of the whitetail's range. Increasing photoperiod triggers antler growth in spring (April in the South and May in the North). In one experiment using artificial lighting, several annual daylight cycles were compressed into one year. Bucks responded by growing as many as three sets of antlers.

Developing antlers are covered with a layer of skin and hair called *velvet*. The fuzzy covering is laced with blood vessels that supply nourishment to the growing antlers. Injuries to developing antlers or to just the velvet can deform them or halt their growth. In extreme cases, one antler may be normal while the other may grow down alongside the head. Injuries can also cause non-typical growth patterns, thicker beams and extra points.

As days become shorter in late summer, male hormone levels rise, causing antlers to stop growing and harden. The velvet then dries and sheds within about 24 hours, usually in late August or early September in the North; September or early October in the South. Bucks in poor condition shed later.

Near the equator, photoperiod varies little and has a minimal effect on the timing of the antler cycle. When a buck's antlers start to grow depends on when the individual was born; the cycle can begin at any time of year.

Decreasing male hormone levels following the rut triggers antler drop, or *casting*. Antlers separate from the deer's head at the pedicles. Northern bucks may drop their antlers as early as December or as late as March; southern bucks, from February to early April. Bucks in poor condition usually cast their antlers earlier than healthy bucks.

Antlered bucks make up a surprisingly small percentage of a typical whitetail population. In early fall, less than 30 percent of the population consists of antlered bucks; after deer season, as little as 10 percent. Many of the bucks have been killed and others have lost their antlers.

How Antlers Develop (timing represents northern whitetail; photos depict different deer)

APRIL. Antler growth originates from the small bony projections just in front of the ears.

JUNE. The sprouting antlers, which are soft and covered with velvet, begin to develop tines.

AUGUST. The antlers have grown to nearly full size, but are still soft and covered with velvet.

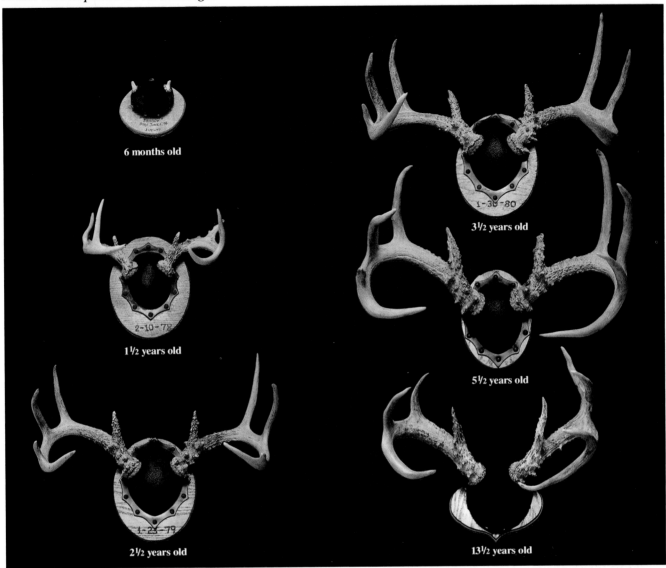

6 months old

1½ years old

2½ years old

3½ years old

5½ years old

13½ years old

CAST ANTLERS from a captive Minnesota whitetail document the typical antler-development pattern. At 6 months of age, the deer had 1-inch spikes; 1½ years, a small 8-point rack; 2½, a rack approaching maximum size; and 3½, a slightly heavier rack. The size and thickness of the rack peaked at 5½ and stayed about the same until 8½. The size of the rack then began to diminish each year, and by 13½, was noticeably smaller.

SEPTEMBER. The fully grown antlers have hardened, and all of the velvet sheds within about a day.

OCTOBER. The antlers are now polished from frequent rubbing on trees and brush.

JANUARY. Antlers are cast as male hormone levels drop. Antlers may not drop off at the same time.

Senses

Honed by a constant struggle for survival, the whitetail's senses of smell, sight and hearing present a formidable challenge to hunters.

Deer researchers know just how elusive whitetails can be. A radio-tagged Wisconsin buck, for instance, was forced out of his home range by opening-day hunters, but returned the next day and spent the remaining 8 days of the season in a wooded ravine. Despite heavy hunting pressure (about 30 hunters per square mile), only a few hunters even saw the deer and they were unable to bag him.

Whitetails routinely evade hunters in much the same manner, and in most cases, hunters assume there are no deer in the area.

Although some outdoor writers have written in very precise terms on what deer can smell, see and hear, there is no scientific basis for such information. Most of what we know about whitetail senses comes from observing the animal and trying to interpret its behavior. The following discussion represents the thinking of prominent deer biologists.

SMELL. Few animals have a better sense of smell than the whitetail. They can detect odors much better and from considerably longer distances than humans. A large portion of the whitetail's brain is devoted to odor reception and interpretation, and its nasal chamber can concentrate odors so they're more identifiable.

Weather conditions affect how well deer detect scents. Steady breezes carry odors long distances, especially in flat, open country. Gusty winds disperse odors, making it hard for deer to locate the source. Dead calm conditions limit the distance at which they can detect intruders. Warming and cooling air can move scents toward or away from deer. In the morning, warming air carries scent uphill; in the evening, cooling air carries it downhill. Humid conditions, including a light drizzle, greatly improve a deer's ability to smell, but heavy rain "washes" odors from the air.

Dense vegetation and rugged terrain stymie a whitetail's sense of smell. And it's usually harder for deer to detect the odor of a hunter above the ground than one at ground level.

VISION. Whitetails have much better dim-light vision than humans. A human's retina is dominated by cones (color receptors); a deer's, rods (light receptors). Rods are about 1,000 times more sensitive to light than cones. A deer's retina also has a layer of reflective pigment, called the *tapetum*. If light passes through the retina without activating the rods, the tapetum bounces it back for a second chance. In addition, the pupil of a deer opens much wider that that of a human, gathering about 9 times more light.

The tapetum causes a deer's eyes to shine at night when struck by a bright light

These adaptations result not only in better vision in dim light or darkness, but also in better peripheral vision and motion detection. The whitetail's habit of standing still when alarmed also helps them detect motion. But deer don't see as clearly as humans, especially at long distances. They're usually unable to identify a motionless hunter.

The whitetail's eyes are on the side of the head, an adaptation which also promotes peripheral vision. Each eye scans nearly 180 degrees, meaning deer can spot movement everywhere except directly to the rear. Looking forward, they have binocular vision and good depth perception over a span of 90 degrees; to the side, monocular vision and poor depth perception.

Although whitetails have some cones in their retina, their ability to see a broad spectrum of colors has never been proven. One study, however, determined that deer can distinguish a fluorescent color from the same nonfluorescent color.

HEARING. A deer's large, cupped external ears gather and, in effect, amplify sound. The ears rotate to detect sounds from any direction. The slight difference in time it takes the sound to reach each ear enables the animal to pinpoint the source.

Short, loud sounds such as gunshots, however, are difficult for whitetails to locate. It's not unusual for a deer to move in the direction of a hunter after a single missed shot.

Deer can hear sounds in about the same frequency range as humans. Hills, heavy cover and rain interfere with a deer's hearing.

WHITETAILS are capable of using all their senses at once to detect danger. This buck has detected the odor of a human and is staring in the direction the odor came from to pick up any movement. At the same time, he has rotated his ears in different directions in an attempt to make out any sound.

COMMUNICATION between members of a group helps whitetails survive. These flagging does have sensed danger and taken flight. The buck has responded by raising its tail and in a moment will join the fleeing does.

Whitetail Communication

Tail wagging means deer are at ease

Whitetails spend most of their lives in groups, a habit that improves their chances of survival. With many eyes and ears on alert, the deer can easily detect an approaching intruder. When one deer senses trouble, it quickly communicates alarm to other group members.

Understanding how whitetails communicate can help you predict their behavior. They relay information to others with visual signs, and sounds such as snorts and grunts.

Tail wagging, casual side-to-side motion without hairs erect, signals no danger. Similar to tail switch-ing in horses and cattle, it is most commonly seen in warmer weather.

Tail flicking, sharp side-to-side motion with the tail horizontal or upright and hairs erect, signals mild alarm. Tail flicking means the deer has sensed something wrong, but doesn't know how to respond. It may stop feeding and raise its head, or lower its head as if to feed and then jerk up again. If the animal doesn't detect anything, it will probably relax and

Tail flicking means something is wrong

Tail flagging signals a high state of alarm

resume normal behavior. But if the disturbance continues, it will take flight.

A whitetail alerts others and quickly brings its group together by holding its tail horizontally or upright with hairs erect, without waving it back and forth. This signal means the deer knows an intruder is close but doesn't know exactly where. It quickly

A horizontal tail means the deer will soon take flight

turns its head in the approximate direction, then stands motionless, moving only its eyes and ears to find the disturbance.

Once the deer is convinced the danger is real, it will *flag* while dashing for safety. The animal bolts away with tail upright, waving it back and forth and expos-

ing the white underside and rump patch. Hair on the tail flares, making it appear larger than it really is. Deer flag less often in dense cover, where signals are not as easily seen by other deer, than in open country.

Vocalizations are not as important in communication as visual signals, but can still help predict behavior. Deer, especially does, sometimes snort when disturbed or alarmed. The short blasts of air or wheezes, made singly or in series, are less common than flagging.

Injured deer sometimes bawl, or make an intense, high-pitched, prolonged call. Bawls warn other deer to flee.

Nervous or alert deer may stamp their front feet

Deer living in groups may stamp their feet when alarmed to warn others. But foot-stamping can be heard for only a short distance.

During the breeding season, deer produce a variety of grunts that vary in tone, duration and intensity. Hunters sometimes imitate these sounds to call whitetails (p. 109). None of these are alarm calls.

RUBBING means the breeding season is underway. As deer rub off bark, they mark the tree with a scent deposit from the preorbital gland at the front of the eye. Rubbing also helps remove velvet from the antlers (inset).

Breeding Behavior

Understanding the mysterious whitetail requires in-depth knowledge of its breeding behavior.

Months before whitetails start to mate, bucks begin to establish dominance. The social hierarchy that results continues through the breeding season, which consists of three phases: prerut, rut, and postrut.

ESTABLISHING DOMINANCE. During the summer, as many as a half-dozen bucks live together; in open habitats such as grasslands or prairies, these groups also contain some does and fawns. The bucks

Summer buck group

determine dominance nonviolently; small ones simply defer to larger ones. As antlers develop, deer with small racks avoid those with large ones.

Grooming and visual intimidation help reveal the pecking order. Subordinate bucks groom dominant

Subordinate buck grooming dominant buck

bucks by licking them around the neck and shoulders. They move out of their paths and avoid eye contact. When bedded, a subordinate buck will never face a dominant buck.

During the summer, bucks avoid settling disputes with their antlers. Because the antlers are still in velvet, they're sensitive and easily injured.

Although they avoid heavy cover, bucks in velvet are secretive and rarely seen. They spend the summer in

SPARRING, which begins at about the same time as rubbing, is usually nonviolent and of short duration. Matches generally last a minute or less, although some go on for several minutes.

open areas where timber or brush won't damage their antlers, and where they can clearly see each other to assess dominance. By summer's end, almost every buck knows his position in the hierarchy.

THE PRERUT. As fall begins, bucks become more antagonistic. Summer groups break up and although the bucks begin to move about more, the dominant bucks stay on their home range, maintaining the social rank.

As soon as their antlers harden (late August or early September in the North; September and early October in the South), bucks begin to make *rubs*, which advertise their presence to other deer. They rake saplings and small trees with their antlers, removing the bark about 2 feet above the ground and depositing scent from their preorbital glands. Early rubs are about 6 inches long and a third of the way around the tree; the tree top is often broken off. Later rubs may be twice as large and much more visible. Bucks commonly rub trees in a cluster or line, but they seldom revisit a rub.

A typical rub tree has smooth bark, few lower branches and is about 1 inch in diameter. But rub trees vary from ½ to 4 inches. Bucks often rub aromatic trees such as pine, cedar and cherry, perhaps because the tree odors enhance the scent. Bigger bucks tend to rub bigger trees.

As soon as bucks start making rubs, they begin to challenge each other by *sparring*. One buck holds its head low and moves toward another, then they press their antlers or foreheads together and begin pushing. Most sparring takes place during daylight hours.

Early sparring matches usually have no winners or losers. The participants soon tire of the shoving and resume what they were doing, often near one another.. This nonviolent sparring reinforces the social rank established during the summer.

Sparring is most common among similar-size bucks, but sometimes a small buck takes on an immovable larger buck who tolerates the pushing briefly, then abruptly ends the contest with a powerful shake of his head. Sometimes bucks spar, push and feint with imaginary partners. And a spike buck may even butt heads with an adult doe.

Later in the prerut, bucks challenge one another more often and more aggressively. As sparring increases, bucks feed less and begin to lose weight. Groups break up and bucks spend their time alone or with one other buck. Most sparring stops once the rut begins.

While bucks are making rubs and sparring, does are busy weaning fawns and feeding heavily to add fat for the winter. They remain in family groups and usually repel advances by bucks. A typical family group includes a matriarch (oldest doe), and her female offspring from the current and previous years. Sometimes a male fawn stays with the group, but as the rut approaches, the adult does drive him away.

THE RUT. The *rut* begins when the first does go into *estrus*, the 24- to 36-hour period when a doe is receptive to breeding. Individual does, however, come into estrus at different times, so the rut usually continues for more than a month. In the North, rutting activity begins in mid-October, peaks in early November, and extends into December.

Because of the milder climate, the rut is less compressed in the South. It starts in late October, peaks in November through early December, and often extends into January. If a doe in estrus is not bred, she comes into estrus again at 28-day intervals through the breeding season.

Weeks before the rut begins, bucks begin to make *scrapes*. They paw at the ground, creating bare patches or shallow depressions that are usually oblong and measure from 1 to 4 feet in length. Rapidly increasing numbers of scrapes is a sure sign the rut is underway.

Most scrapes are made beneath a low, spreading branch or sapling where there is little ground cover. Typically, a buck makes several lines or clusters of scrapes within his home range, increasing the odds that does will find them. The scrapes are almost always near rubs. Bucks usually make scrapes and rubs where they're easily found – near feeding areas, at trail intersections or along roads, fence rows or edges of clearings.

A buck marks rubs and scrapes with his own scent, leaving a "calling card" for does, and reinforcing his

SCRAPES are characterized by an oblong patch of pawed ground beneath an overhanging branch or sapling. A buck pulls the branch down with his mouth, often breaking the tip in the process (inset).

social rank. He rubs his head against the rub tree and licks or rubs the branch or sapling overhanging the scrape. If he cannot find any suitable vegetation to rub against, he'll use practically any object he can find, such as a fence post.

He also marks scrapes with urine, the strongest and most important scent. He squats and urinates down his legs into his tarsal glands. Then he rubs the tarsals together, squeezing old, strong-smelling urine into the scrape. This process, called *rub-urination*, produces an odor so intense even humans can smell

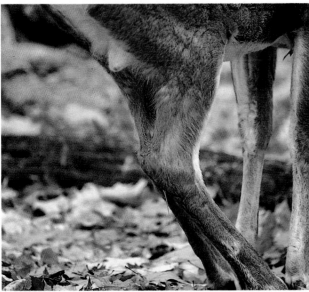
Rub-urination

it. Interdigital glands between the hoof sections may leave additional scent. The odor from each marking lasts several days, and bucks repeatedly return to mark the same scrapes.

Does also routinely investigate these scrapes and, on occasion, make scrapes of their own. When a doe is ready to breed, she urinates in scrapes as a signal to the buck.

During the peak of scraping activity, bucks sometimes make "false" scrapes, which are smaller than normal and not beneath an overhanging branch. Apparently, the buck instinctively feels the location is poor, or he abandons the scrape in the height of sexual excitement.

Your chances of bagging a trophy buck are never better than during the rut. Bucks are preoccupied with breeding activity, so they lose their normal caution and become mistake-prone. They also move more during the rut than at any other time of year as they freshen and check their scrapes and look for does. Their movements peak a few hours before dusk.

Does move more during the rut too. Shortly before estrus, they begin pacing at night; this restlessness increases their nighttime movements to almost 30

times their normal total, although most of it takes place within a small area of their home range. In one Michigan study, a pre-estrus doe paced over 20 miles in a single night.

Actual breeding activity begins with a courtship ritual, which is initiated when a buck catches a whiff of a doe in estrus. He sniffs the doe's trail and gives chase with his neck extended, head low and chin up-turned. More than one buck may take up the chase, but the dominant buck follows closest to the doe. He makes low, long grunts, snorts and wheezes during the chase.

A buck sometime stops to sniff urine left by the doe. He extends his neck, holds his snout slightly upward and curls back his upper lip to close the nasal cham-

Lip curling

ber, intensifying the urine odor to help determine the stage of estrus.

When a buck approaches within 10 or 15 yards, the doe flees, unless she is ready to breed. The buck may give chase, but only for 100 yards or so.

Pre-estrus does avoid dominant bucks

31

A doe in estrus allows a dominant buck to approach

Typical antler threat

Tolerance between bucks vanishes during courtship. If a small buck gets within about 30 yards of a doe during the chase, the dominant buck will lower his head, stare, tip his antlers, drop his ears and raise his body hair to scare the smaller buck away. But they will rarely fight, because rank was determined before the rut. A big buck seldom chases a smaller one very far; his main concern is staying with the doe.

If a small buck curls his lip where a doe urinated, the dominant buck will drive him away, then begin lip curling in the same spot.

Sometimes bucks of equal body and antler size square off and neither backs down, so an antler battle ensues. Bucks circle one another before charging and clashing antlers. After 5 to 10 seconds of intense shoving and twisting, the dominant buck stands his ground and the loser retreats. Occasionally, the antlers become locked together and both bucks struggle to the death. Only in very rare instances do bucks kill each other when their antlers aren't locked.

Deer may die of exhaustion should their antlers become locked

Eventually, a doe in estrus allows a breeding buck to approach. Before copulation, the buck stays near the doe, feeding and bedding with her for a day or more. This behavior is called *tending*. He may sniff her rump and feign a chase to test her intent to breed. When she is ready, the buck mounts her. He may continue tending her for several more days, defending

Frequency of Rubbing, Scraping and Breeding

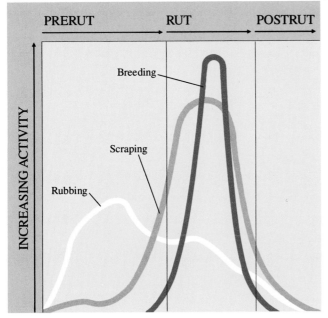

RUBBING signals the start of the prerut. Rubbing activity peaks in the middle to late stage of the prerut, then tapers off through the postrut. Heavy scraping activity begins about three weeks before the start of the rut, peaks in the middle of the rut (at the height of breeding activity), then declines rapidly following the rut.

her from other bucks and sometimes breeding her several times while she's in estrus.

If another buck approaches a tending buck, the dominant animal assumes the same threatening posture used during courtship (opposite page) to chase the subordinate buck away.

After he finishes tending, a dominant buck will pursue other does as they come into estrus; he will court, tend and breed with as many females as possible, including adults, yearlings, and even fawns.

By the end of the rut, practically all does capable of breeding are bred.

POSTRUT. As male hormone levels diminish and bucks can no longer find any does in estrus, rubbing and scraping gradually diminishes. In the North, harsh weather further limits this activity. Most bucks lose their antlers within a month after the rut ends, although bucks in good condition may carry them several months longer.

When breeding has been completed, bucks begin feeding more heavily to regain lost weight. Does are in better condition after the rut, but they too feed heavily to add fat reserves for the upcoming winter.

Toward the end of the gestation period, which lasts about 6½ months, does leave their family groups and go off by themselves to deliver, usually in May or

How Latitude Affects Timing of the Rut

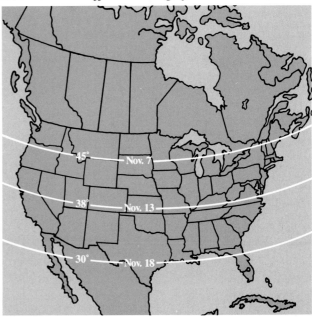

THE PEAK of the rut varies only a few weeks from north to south. At 45 degrees North, the peak is about November 7; at 38 degrees North, November 13; and at 30 degrees North, November 18. However, these dates may vary by several weeks because of climate. The warmer the climate, the longer the rut tends to last.

Triplets aren't unusual in agricultural areas

June. On good range, adult does and yearlings generally give birth to twins, and sometimes triplets. Up to 60 percent of female fawns become pregnant; they usually have single births.

On poor range, adult females may have single or twin births. Yearlings may not become pregnant, and if they do, they have single births. Female fawns will not become pregnant, even if they are bred.

After giving birth, the doe remains isolated from the family group as she nurses the fawns, drives other deer away from them and decoys predators. If you see a fawn by itself, don't assume it's abandoned. A doe with twins intentionally keeps them apart so a predator doesn't kill them both. After about a month, the doe and fawns join the family group.

CONTROLLED BURNS, fires set at the right time of year and carefully monitored, remove the forest canopy so sunlight can reach plants on the forest floor. Fires also return nutrients stored in vegetation back to the soil.

Whitetail Conservation

"There is such infinite Herds that the whole country seems but one continued park." – *Thomas Ashe, referring to whitetail sightings in South Carolina in 1682*

Before the settlers arrived, an estimated 30 million whitetails inhabited what is now the United States and Canada. But as settlers pursued them for food and market hunters slaughtered them with snares, traps and set guns, the deer population underwent a disastrous decline. By 1900, only 400,000 whitetails remained.

What happened since 1900, however, is perhaps the most dramatic success story in conservation history. Through a massive cooperative effort by concerned sportsmen and wildlife managers, market hunting was outlawed, sport-hunting regulations established, and habitat improvement programs initiated. These efforts have now rebuilt the whitetail population to 20 million.

But the conservation battle is far from over. Whitetails in many parts of their range now face a threat even more serious than uncontrolled hunting: loss of critical habitat.

Southern pine forests, for example, often develop a dense canopy which prevents sunlight from reaching the forest floor and stimulating the needed plant growth. Here, fire plays a major role. Controlled burns remove the heavy overstory, allowing sunlight to reach the ground and creating openings that supply the "edge" habitat so critical to deer.

In northern forests, openings are usually created by logging or applying herbicides, but in some cases controlled burns are also used.

In certain farmland regions, deer suffer from a lack of forests, wetlands or other cover to protect them from winter blizzards. Conservation agencies and private groups purchase woodlots, cattail marshes, grasslands and woodlands along streams. They also plant trees to create woodlots and shelter belts, mul-

These seedlings will make good whitetail cover in a few years

tiple tree rows that break the winter winds. Where food is in short supply, they plant wildlife food plots, usually corn or other agricultural crops.

In Western grasslands, whitetails often share their range with livestock. Wildlife managers and agricultural agencies must cooperate to make arrangements, such as cattle grazing rotations, that will allow deer and livestock to coexist. In some cases, water is the key to maintaining a deer herd. Conservation agencies maintain water holes so the animals can live where a lack of water would otherwise limit survival.

AFTER the burn, young vegetation begins to sprout almost immediately. Eventually, a dense layer of underbrush, grasses and forbs develops, providing whitetails with cover and an abundant supply of food.

Deer often become too numerous in suburban and agricultural areas. They cause traffic accidents, damage gardens and shrubbery and eat valuable crops. Where hunting is allowed, these problems are not as severe. The remaining deer can be diverted

Food plots keep deer in good shape all winter

from problem areas with special food plots, fences or chemical repellents.

Despite the importance of hunting as a deer-management tool, increasing antihunting sentiment fostered by animal-rights and some environmental groups poses a threat to the sport. Many such organizations are well organized, well funded and have considerable legislative clout.

Many nonhunters do not realize that practically all whitetail restoration efforts were financed by sales of hunting licences and taxes on hunting equipment. Ongoing management programs also depend on revenue from hunters.

Poachers and irresponsible hunters who trespass on private land, shoot from vehicles and take more deer

than the law allows only fuel the antihunting movement. Many states have established programs that encourage responsible hunters to report any violations they witness. These programs have proven very effective, greatly increasing the number of arrests.

As a hunter, you are a vital part of the whitetail conservation effort. Always cooperate with wildlife agencies when they request that you register your deer or fill out a questionnaire after the season. The data they gather helps them determine herd structure

Data from hunters helps wildlife managers set seasons

and harvest rate, information needed to set harvest quotas for the next season.

Participating in a sportsman's club or other conservation organization can also pay dividends. Many clubs assist wildlife managers on habitat-development and emergency winter-feeding projects. And it helps to have a united voice when dealing with state legislatures on deer-related issues.

Equipment

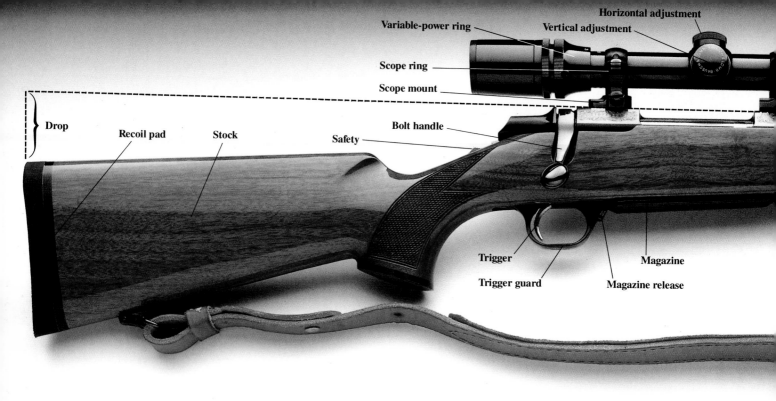

Horizontal adjustment
Variable-power ring
Vertical adjustment
Scope ring
Scope mount
Drop
Recoil pad
Stock
Safety
Bolt handle
Trigger
Trigger guard
Magazine
Magazine release

Rifles & Ammunition

Choosing the right rifle makes your hunt more enjoyable and boosts your odds for success. Consider fit, sights, weight, action and caliber.

FIT. A properly fitting gun helps you shoot more accurately. To check the fit, bring the firearm to your shoulder. A stock that's too long will catch in your armpit, especially if you're wearing a heavy jacket.

If the stock is too short, the scope may strike your eyebrow when you shoot, giving you a "scope bite."

Stock lengths vary among different rifle models, but a given model is generally available in one length only. A gunsmith can easily shorten or lengthen a stock for you.

Another consideration is *drop* (see photo above). With your cheek pressed firmly against the stock, your shooting eye should automatically line up with the sights. Too much drop will prevent you from plac-

Popular Rifle Sights

OPEN sights have a front post which must be centered in the notched rear sight. But even the flat, leaf-style type shown covers up some of the target and is hard to line up.

PEEP sights with large rear apertures make it easy to find and track deer, even in heavy cover. With the target centered through the peep, line up the front bead on the vital area.

4-PLEX reticles, the most popular type, help you get on target quickly. Your eye can easily follow the thick, black lines to the fine crosshairs in the center of the scope.

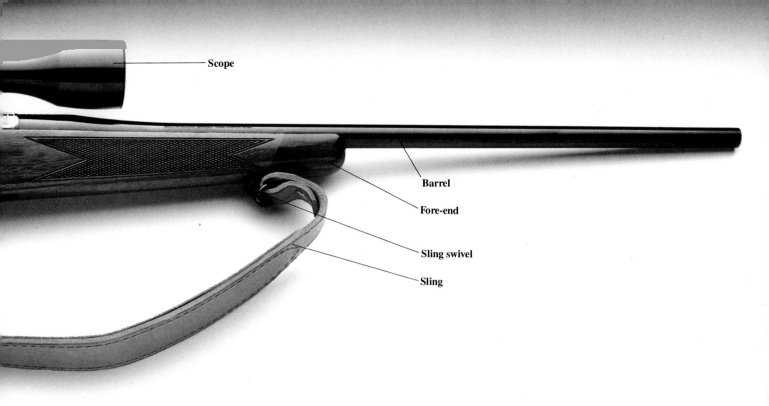

Scope

Barrel

Fore-end

Sling swivel

Sling

ing your cheek on the stock, and recoil could slam the stock against your cheekbone.

The results of a poor fit may be painful, causing you to flinch and making accurate shooting impossible. If you lack the experience to tell when a gun does or doesn't fit, seek the help of an expert at a gun or sport shop.

SIGHTS. If you hunt in heavy cover where short shots are the rule, buy a low-power scope or a peep sight with a large aperture. You can aim either one

quickly and accurately. Variable-power scopes, about 1.5x-4.5x or 2x-7x, are ideal.

Open sights, standard on most rifles, are hard to line up accurately and quickly. They are the most difficult to master.

WEIGHT. Most hunting rifles weigh between 6 and 9 pounds. Lighter guns are more comfortable to carry; heavy ones kick less, are easier to hold steady and are a better choice for stand-hunting and taking long shots.

POST reticles work well for heavy cover and moving deer; the post is easy to see but covers a lot of the target on long shots. A wide-angle lens helps find and track moving deer.

DOT reticles have a small black dot that quickly takes your eye to the junction of the crosshairs. At long ranges, use a scope with a very small dot so it won't obscure the target.

CROSSHAIR reticles are best suited to precision shooting at long range. But the fine wires may be hard to see in dim light or heavy shadow, and tough to keep on a moving target.

Use a sling to safely tote your rifle when not hunting. Select one with detachable swivels so you can remove the sling when still-hunting (p. 85); otherwise it might get in the way.

ACTION. The action you select will depend on your need for a quick second shot, accuracy requirements and personal preference. However, not all calibers are available in each type of action.

Actions range from sturdy single-shots to reliable, accurate bolt-actions to fast-shooting lever actions, pumps and semi-automatics.

If you will be hunting in sub-zero temperatures, remove all dirt and oil from your gun's action. Normal gun oil thickens and may cause your gun to jam. Most actions will function well without lubricants for a short time. But if you do a lot of shooting in cold weather, lubricate the action lightly with a graphite or other cold-weather lubricant.

CARTRIDGES. For whitetails, a cartridge should deliver at least 900 foot-pounds of energy at the point of impact (see table at right). Most states and provinces have minimum cartridge specifications for whitetail hunting.

Medium-caliber, high-velocity cartridges are the best choice for deer hunting. Common cartridges in this class are the .30-06 Springfield, .308 Winchester, .270 Winchester and 7mm Remington Magnum. Bullets should weigh at least 130 grains. Fine accuracy, plenty of power and flat trajectories make these cartridges suitable in any cover, and for shots as long as 300 yards.

If you're sensitive to recoil, choose high-velocity cartridges in smaller calibers, such as the 6mm Remington, .243 Winchester, .257 Roberts and .25-06 Remington. These bullets should weigh a minimum of 100 grains. You can expect tack-driving accuracy, flat trajectory and adequate power for deer out to 250 yards.

For nearly a century, whitetail hunters relied on low-velocity cartridges and bullets in calibers such as the .30-30 Winchester, .35 Remington, .300 Savage, .351 Winchester and .444 Marlin. But ballistics tests have proven that these reputed "brush busters" are actually deflected more by brush than high-velocity bullets. These cartridges are best used at ranges less than 150 yards because of their low velocity and rainbow trajectory.

Pointed bullets retain velocity and energy better at long range, have flatter trajectories and are less affected by wind drift than are round-nosed bullets. However, only round-nosed bullets should be used in rifles with tubular magazines. Recoil could cause a pointed bullet to detonate the cartridge in front of it.

RIFLE ACTIONS include: (1) Bolt actions, which are sturdy, reliable and accurate. They're the most popular repeaters, and are available in the widest selection of calibers, weights and barrel lengths. (2) Single shots are also sturdy, reliable, accurate and easy to handle. (3) Lever actions allow quick follow-up shots, so they're most popular in areas where you have to make quick shots in heavy brush. (4) Semi-automatics fire most rapidly, and the gas action minimizes recoil. (5) Pumps can be fired almost as rapidly as semi-automatics. Both are heavy to carry and have more moving parts than other action types, so they're more likely to jam when dirty or cold.

How to Interpret a Ballistics Table

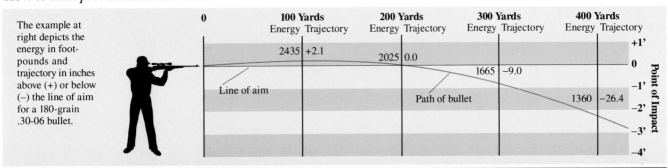

The example at right depicts the energy in foot-pounds and trajectory in inches above (+) or below (–) the line of aim for a 180-grain .30-06 bullet.

	0	100 Yards Energy Trajectory	200 Yards Energy Trajectory	300 Yards Energy Trajectory	400 Yards Energy Trajectory	Point of Impact
		2435 +2.1	2025 0.0	1665 –9.0	1360 –26.4	

Line of aim   Path of bullet

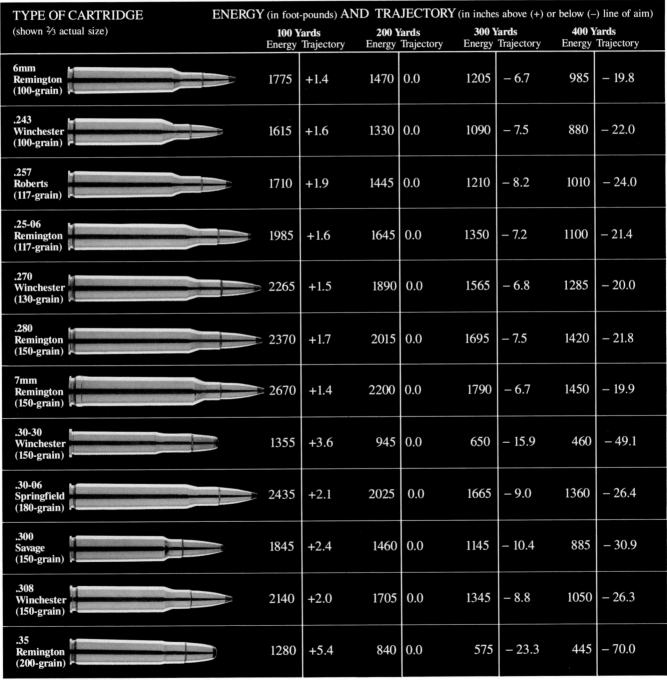

TYPE OF CARTRIDGE (shown ⅔ actual size)		ENERGY (in foot-pounds) AND TRAJECTORY (in inches above (+) or below (–) line of aim)							
		100 Yards		200 Yards		300 Yards		400 Yards	
		Energy	Trajectory	Energy	Trajectory	Energy	Trajectory	Energy	Trajectory
6mm Remington (100-grain)		1775	+1.4	1470	0.0	1205	– 6.7	985	– 19.8
.243 Winchester (100-grain)		1615	+1.6	1330	0.0	1090	– 7.5	880	– 22.0
.257 Roberts (117-grain)		1710	+1.9	1445	0.0	1210	– 8.2	1010	– 24.0
.25-06 Remington (117-grain)		1985	+1.6	1645	0.0	1350	– 7.2	1100	– 21.4
.270 Winchester (130-grain)		2265	+1.5	1890	0.0	1565	– 6.8	1285	– 20.0
.280 Remington (150-grain)		2370	+1.7	2015	0.0	1695	– 7.5	1420	– 21.8
7mm Remington (150-grain)		2670	+1.4	2200	0.0	1790	– 6.7	1450	– 19.9
.30-30 Winchester (150-grain)		1355	+3.6	945	0.0	650	– 15.9	460	– 49.1
.30-06 Springfield (180-grain)		2435	+2.1	2025	0.0	1665	– 9.0	1360	– 26.4
.300 Savage (150-grain)		1845	+2.4	1460	0.0	1145	– 10.4	885	– 30.9
.308 Winchester (150-grain)		2140	+2.0	1705	0.0	1345	– 8.8	1050	– 26.3
.35 Remington (200-grain)		1280	+5.4	840	0.0	575	– 23.3	445	– 70.0

BALLISTICS TABLES help you select the best caliber and cartridge for your hunting. At 300 yards, for example, a 6mm Remington hits only 6.7 inches low and delivers 1205 foot-pounds of energy, plenty to kill a deer; a .35 Remington hits 23.3 inches low and delivers only 575 foot-pounds, not enough for a clean kill.

Shotguns & Ammunition

Shotguns and slugs are widely used for deer hunting in agricultural or densely populated areas; many states and provinces do not allow rifle hunting in

If you don't have a slug barrel, use a smoothbore gun with rifled slugs, although accuracy will suffer. Generally, the less choke, the better. Rifled choke tubes are available for some smoothbore barrels and cost substantially less than interchangeable rifled barrels. Most double-barrels handle slugs poorly, with each barrel shooting to a different spot.

While barrels with rifling are best for slugs, buckshot patterns better with a smooth bore. To make sure enough pellets hit the vital area of the deer, use a 10- or 12-gauge gun with a full choke.

SIGHTS. It's impossible to shoot accurately for much distance with just the front bead of a smoothbore barrel. You can buy open sights that temporarily

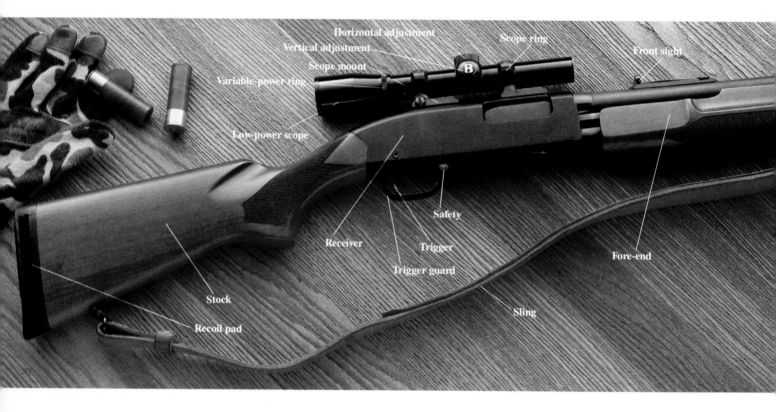

these locales. Some southern states also permit the use of shotguns with buckshot.

The ideal shotgun for whitetail hunting has a rifled barrel and special sights. Proper ammunition is important too.

BARRELS. Rifled barrels shoot slugs more accurately than smoothbores. Rifling spins and stabilizes the slug, allowing shots at deer out to 100 yards. Rifled barrels are available for many popular brands of pump and semi-automatic shotguns. The barrels are typically 20 to 26 inches long with front and back sights and no choke. You can easily switch them with smoothbore barrels. Consult a gun dealer to determine if a rifled slug barrel is made for your shotgun.

attach to the rib, receiver or barrel without marring the finish of your gun. However, low-power scopes offer the greatest accuracy.

With a specially designed slug gun, you can easily mount a scope on the receiver; most are tapped to accept screws for a scope mount. With a smoothbore, consult a gunsmith for scope-mounting options. You may be able to mount your scope to the side of the receiver using the holes for the trigger-assembly pins. This way, you won't have to drill more holes.

AMMUNITION. Slug guns and ammunition are available in all popular gauges; 12 gauge is the most widely used. Never use anything less than 20 gauge for hunting deer.

SLUGS include: (1) Sabot-type, with a plastic sleeve (the Sabot) that encases an elongated projectile. Sabots are very accurate and ballistically superior to (2) Foster-style slugs, which have a cup-shaped, nose-heavy design.

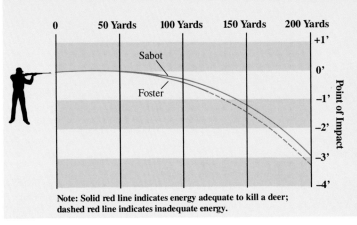

Note: Solid red line indicates energy adequate to kill a deer; dashed red line indicates inadequate energy.

PERFORMANCE comparisons show the Sabot-style slug has a slightly flatter trajectory and more energy than the Foster style at long distances. At close range, there is little difference between the two.

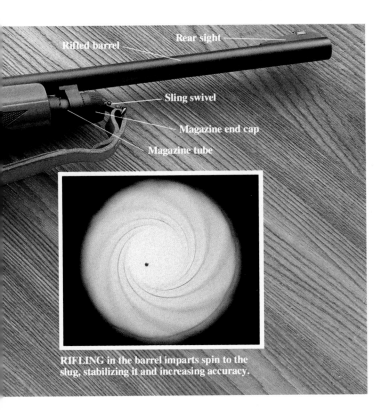

RIFLING in the barrel imparts spin to the slug, stabilizing it and increasing accuracy.

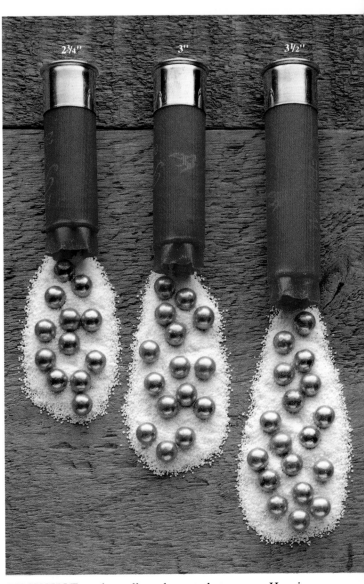

BUCKSHOT works well on deer at close range. Heavier loads are better than light ones, not because they increase your range, but because they give you a denser pattern. A 12-gauge, 2¾-inch load of 00 buck, for instance, has 12 pellets; a 3-inch load, 15; a 3½-inch load, 18.

Variations in slug design can affect accuracy. Most shotguns are a little more accurate at long range with Sabot (pronounced say-bo)-style slugs than the traditional Foster style (see photo above).

Performance of slugs in your gun will vary between brands because of differences in slug diameter. To determine which brand is most accurate in your gun, fire 3-shot groups with several slug brands at the maximum distance you usually shoot at deer.

Buckshot sizes 00 and 000 are most effective for whitetail hunting. Shoot different brands of buckshot at 30 yards to determine which produces the tightest pattern in your shotgun. Few guns shoot a tight enough pattern for a clean kill beyond 30 yards.

Muzzleloaders

With a "smokepole," you'd better make your first shot count. Most muzzleloaders are capable of only one shot and all are slow to reload, but good ones are accurate out to 125 yards.

Many states have muzzleloader-only seasons, allowing you to extend your time afield and escape the hunting pressure of regular firearms seasons.

Hunters can choose between caplocks and flintlocks (see below). Although traditionalists often prefer flintlocks, caplocks are less likely to misfire.

Most muzzleloader hunters prefer .50- or .54-caliber rifles for whitetails. Check regulations to find out which calibers are legal in your state.

Muzzleloader projectiles include: round balls, conical bullets and Sabot/pistol bullets. Some states allow only the round ball, which is accurate but loses energy more rapidly than the others. Conicals are as accurate as round balls but much heavier, so they retain far more downrange energy. Sabots are very accurate in barrels with the proper degree of rifling twist, and also maintain excellent downrange energy due to their superior aerodynamic design.

For Sabots and conicals, use a fast-twist barrel (about one full twist in 32 inches); for round balls, a slower twist (about one full twist in 66 inches).

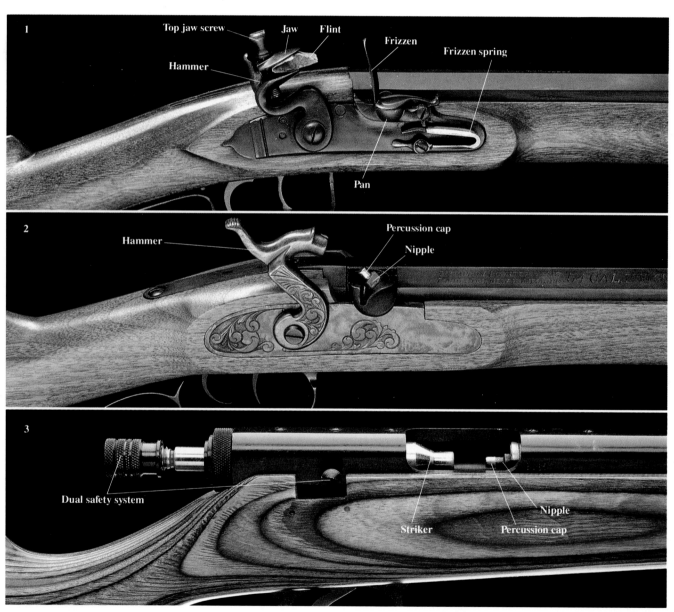

ACTIONS include: (1) flintlock, in which a flint in the hammer strikes the frizzen, sending sparks through the flash hole and igniting the priming powder, which in turn sets off the main powder charge. In a (2) caplock, the hammer hits a percussion cap, sending a spark through the nipple and flash hole to the powder charge. In an (3) in-line-ignition caplock, the striker, nipple, flash channel and powder charge are all in a direct line. This design is most reliable because it reduces ignition time and seldom misfires, and it's safest because of the dual safeties.

Black powder, the traditional choice among muzzle-loader hunters, is classified according to the size of the individual powder granules. The finest is FFFFg, used for priming flintlocks. The coarsest is Fg, used primarily in black-powder shotguns. Most large-caliber rifles perform best with FFg, smaller calibers with FFFg.

Some hunters, however, prefer Pyrodex to black powder because it doesn't cause as much corrosion. Pyrodex also comes in a selection of granule sizes, but only RS (rifle-shotgun) should be used in muzzle-loading rifles.

To "work up a load," shoot a series of three-shot groups, increasing powder charge in 5-grain increments to determine the best powder charge for the projectile you're shooting. Always follow the manufacturers' guidelines and never exceed their recommended maximum charges. If you're not satisfied with the accuracy, repeat the procedure with a different type of projectile.

Telescopic sights, which increase accuracy, and double-barrels, which permit a quick second shot, are prohibited in some states.

Muzzleloaders foul quickly; powder residue builds up rapidly inside the barrel and flashhole, attracting moisture and promoting rust. Many hunters run a patch through the bore between each shot. Never allow a muzzleloader to stand overnight after it has been shot. Clean thoroughly using a cleaning solution or hot water.

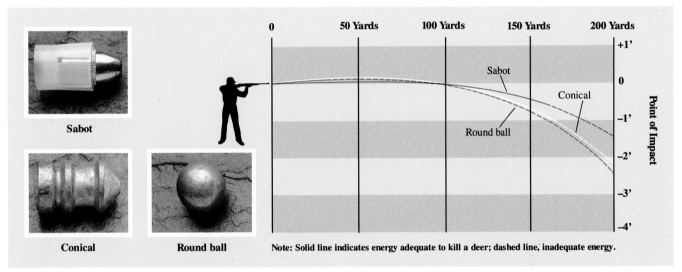

PERFORMANCE of muzzleloader bullets differs greatly. The Sabot has a slightly flatter trajectory than the conical, but the conical has a little more energy at long range. Both are ballistically superior to the round ball. However, some states allow the use of only the round ball for deer hunting.

EQUIPMENT for the hunt includes: (1) quickloads, which make loading fast and easy; (2) in-line capper, to hold spare caps and put a cap on the nipple; (3) bullet starter; (4) nipple wrench; (5) nipple pick, to keep the flashhole open; (6) spare nipple; (7) bullet puller, should a bullet stick in the barrel; (8) patch puller; (9) cleaning rod to which the bullet and patch pullers attach (you can also use a T-handle with your ramrod); (10) possibles bag for above items. Flintlock shooters need (11) extra flint instead of caps and (12) priming powder.

How to Use a Quickload

SUPPLIES for loading quickloads include: (1) powder, (2) powder measure, bullets such as (3) conicals, (4) Sabots and (5) round balls. The round balls are used with a (6) patch that must be lubricated with (7) patch lube. If the conicals are not pre-lubed, apply (8) bullet grease.

MAKE a quickload by removing one cap, pushing in the bullet and replacing the cap. Remove the other cap, pour in the powder then replace the cap.

POUR powder down the barrel after removing the cap. Point the muzzle away from your face to prevent injury should the powder accidentally ignite.

STRIKE the starter with your palm after removing the other cap and centering the bullet. Tamp the bullet an inch or two down the barrel.

SEAT the bullet firmly on the powder, using the ramrod. For proper seating each time, etch a mark on the ramrod at muzzle level.

Equipment for Cleaning Muzzleloaders

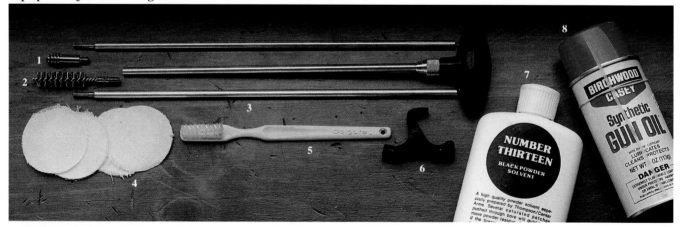

CLEANING EQUIPMENT includes: (1) cleaning jag and (2) bore brush, which attach to (3) cleaning rod (or ramrod with T-handle); (4) bore patches, which fit onto cleaning jag; (5) toothbrush or pipe cleaner to clean the nipple;

(6) barrel key puller; (7) cleaning solution; and (8) gun oil for lightly oiling the bore and all other metal parts after cleaning. You'll also need the nipple wrench and patch puller on page 45.

Handguns

Handguns increase the challenge of hunting white-tails and allow many disabled hunters to enjoy the sport. But handguns lack the velocity, range and accuracy of high-powered rifles, so you must be an expert shot and recognize a handgun's limitations when shooting at deer.

The most accurate and powerful handguns are long-barreled, bolt-action or break-action single shots chambered for rifle cartridges such as the .30-30 and .35 Remington.

Revolvers chambered for pistol cartridges such as the .454 Casull, .44 Magnum, .41 Magnum and .357 Magnum can fire several shots without reloading, but are less powerful. In fact, the .454 Casull and .44 Magnum produce only about half the energy of common deer-rifle loads. Check your state's regulations to learn which calibers are legal. Though many states allow use of the .357, it lacks sufficient energy for consistent clean kills.

Becoming an expert pistol shot requires a great deal of practice. The powerful cartridges used for hunting are expensive and produce so much recoil that practicing can be a painful chore. To save money and develop a steady hand, shoot loads with lighter bullets and powder charges when target practicing. Switch to hunting loads and be sure to sight-in again just before the deer season.

If you're trying out a handgun with the idea of buying it, remember to use full-power hunting loads. Otherwise, you may find that your new sidearm kicks like a cannon, making it difficult to shoot comfortably and accurately.

To improve your handgun's accuracy, equip it with a 1x to 4x pistol scope, assuming they are legal where you hunt.

Bolt-action repeater

Break-action single shot

Revolver

Note: Solid red line indicates energy adequate to kill a deer; dashed red line, inadequate energy.

PERFORMANCE of rifle loads shot in pistols is superior to that of even the most powerful pistol loads. At 100 yards, the .30-30 is dead-on and delivers 1039 foot-pounds of energy. At the same distance, the .44 hits 6.5 inches low and delivers only 543 foot-pounds.

Archery Equipment

Bowhunting for whitetails was once the province of a few highly skilled archers. But new designs have made the bow easier to shoot accurately and opened the door to any archer willing to put in time at the target range.

Bowhunters enjoy longer seasons than gun hunters and, during archery-only seasons, face considerably less competition for prime hunting spots. Also, many hunters relish the challenge of hunting with a bow and arrow.

Today, more than 80 percent of whitetail bowhunters use compound bows. Available with solid-fiberglass or laminated-wood limbs, compounds use cams and pulleys to shoot arrows faster than longbows or recurves, resulting in a flatter trajectory and delivering more energy to the target.

Most compound bows reduce draw weight at full draw by 50 to 65 percent. This *let-off* allows you to hold a powerful bow much longer at full draw, an important feature when you're waiting for a whitetail to move into position for a clear shot. A compound bow set at 60-pound draw weight with 50 percent let-off, for instance, requires only 30 pounds of pull to hold at full draw.

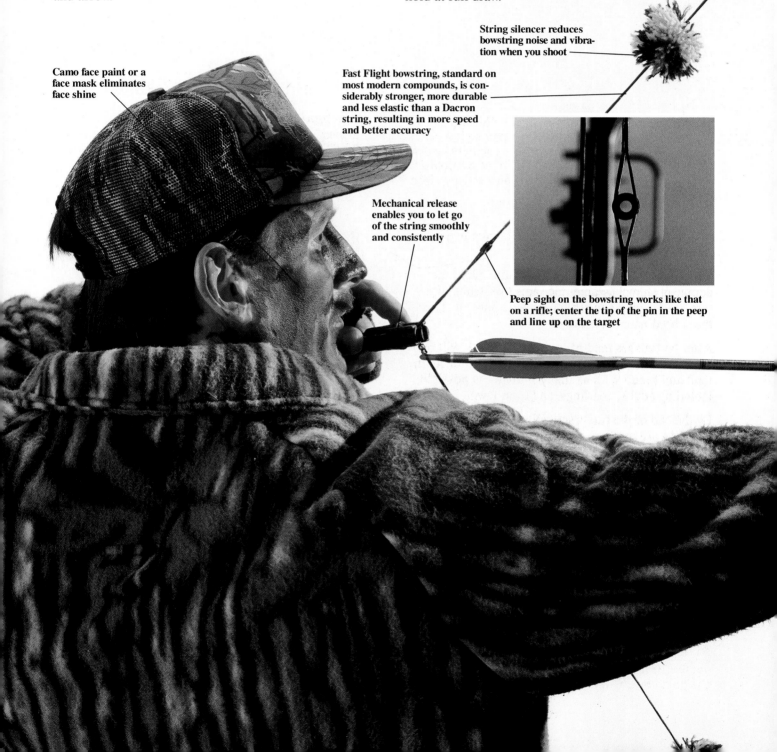

Camo face paint or a face mask eliminates face shine

Fast Flight bowstring, standard on most modern compounds, is considerably stronger, more durable and less elastic than a Dacron string, resulting in more speed and better accuracy

String silencer reduces bowstring noise and vibration when you shoot

Mechanical release enables you to let go of the string smoothly and consistently

Peep sight on the bowstring works like that on a rifle; center the tip of the pin in the peep and line up on the target

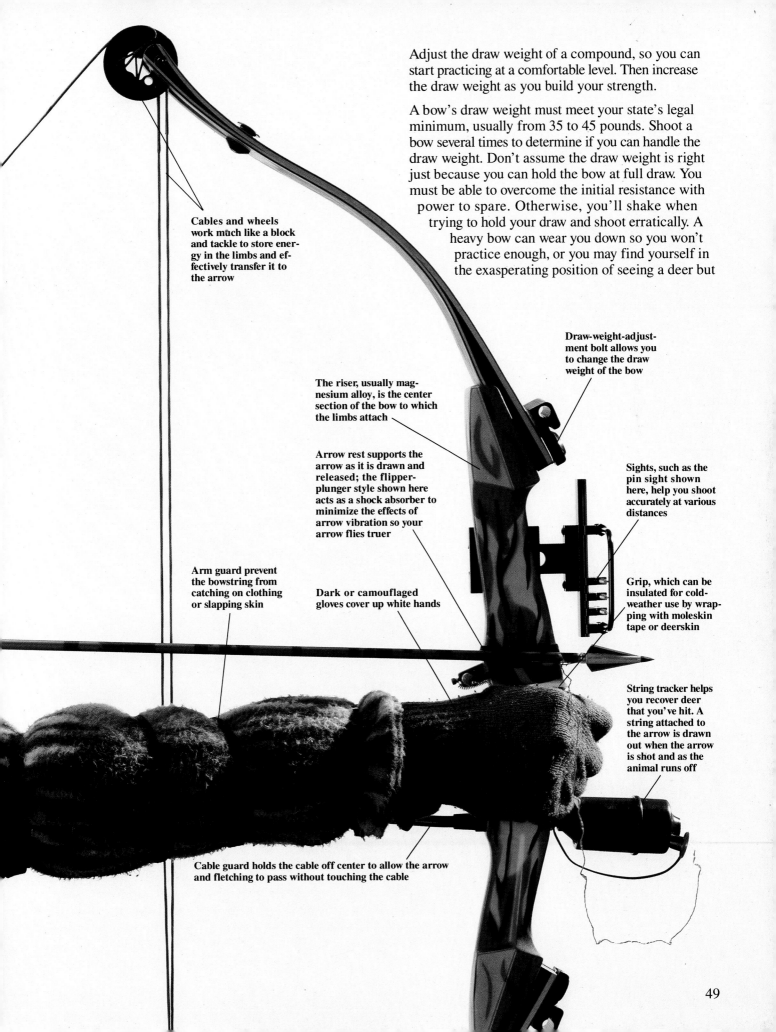

Adjust the draw weight of a compound, so you can start practicing at a comfortable level. Then increase the draw weight as you build your strength.

A bow's draw weight must meet your state's legal minimum, usually from 35 to 45 pounds. Shoot a bow several times to determine if you can handle the draw weight. Don't assume the draw weight is right just because you can hold the bow at full draw. You must be able to overcome the initial resistance with power to spare. Otherwise, you'll shake when trying to hold your draw and shoot erratically. A heavy bow can wear you down so you won't practice enough, or you may find yourself in the exasperating position of seeing a deer but

Cables and wheels work much like a block and tackle to store energy in the limbs and effectively transfer it to the arrow

Draw-weight-adjustment bolt allows you to change the draw weight of the bow

The riser, usually magnesium alloy, is the center section of the bow to which the limbs attach

Arrow rest supports the arrow as it is drawn and released; the flipper-plunger style shown here acts as a shock absorber to minimize the effects of arrow vibration so your arrow flies truer

Sights, such as the pin sight shown here, help you shoot accurately at various distances

Grip, which can be insulated for cold-weather use by wrapping with moleskin tape or deerskin

Arm guard prevent the bowstring from catching on clothing or slapping skin

Dark or camouflaged gloves cover up white hands

String tracker helps you recover deer that you've hit. A string attached to the arrow is drawn out when the arrow is shot and as the animal runs off

Cable guard holds the cable off center to allow the arrow and fletching to pass without touching the cable

being unable to draw the bow and make any shot at all.

If the draw length (see photo) is too short, it's impossible to pull the string back to your anchor point; too long, and you won't be able to draw the bow to full power.

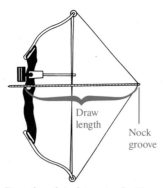

Draw length is determined with a calibrated draw-check arrow. Draw the arrow to your anchor point (alongside your cheek); your draw length is the distance between the bottom of the nock groove and the far side of the bow.

To shoot more accurately, most bowhunters use pin sights (p. 49), mounted just above the arrow rest. Pins are commonly set for 10, 20 and 30 yards.

Despite the popularity of compounds, some hunters still prefer traditional bows. Longbows and recurve bows are lighter and quieter than compounds, but require more practice to shoot accurately.

Longbows have long limbs that store and release energy. Recurves have double-flexed limbs that store even more energy with less length. Most recurves and longbows are made of fiberglass-laminated wood, although some longbows are solid wood. Either bow with a 60-pound draw weight requires 60 pounds of pull to hold at full draw – too much for most hunters to hold more than a few seconds.

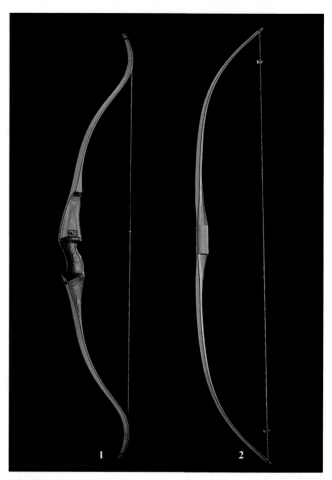

OTHER BOW TYPES include: (1) recurve and (2) longbow, or straight-limb bow, preferred by some traditionalists. Recurves deliver more energy for a given draw weight than do longbows.

Common Quiver Types

BOW quivers are the most popular style. They hold arrows securely and within easy reach, but can affect accuracy at longer ranges.

BACK quivers, many of which double as small daypacks, hold 4 to 8 arrows vertically so they can easily be extracted when needed.

HIP quivers are most popular with target archers. But many bowhunters also like to have their spare arrows so easily accessible.

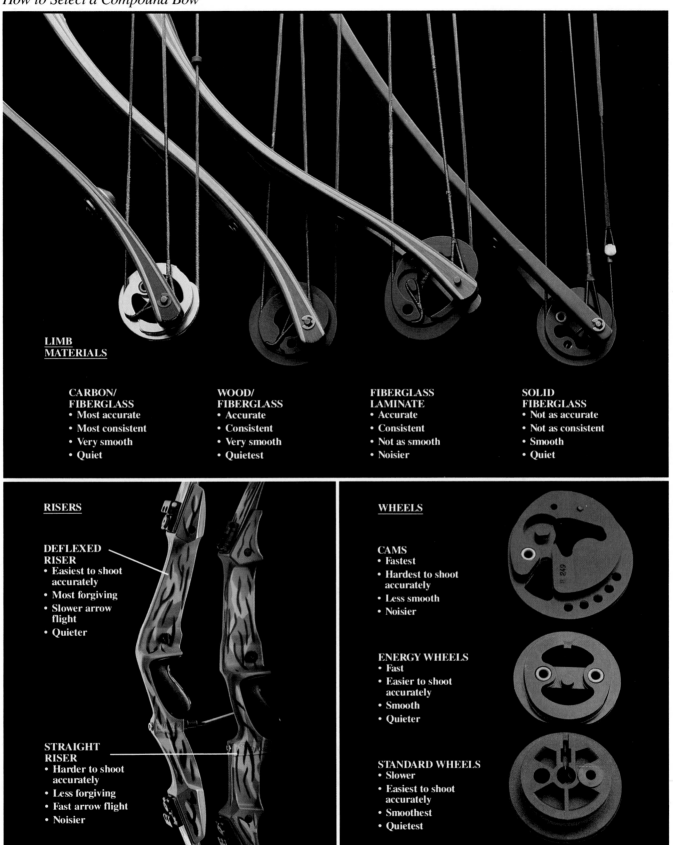

LIMB MATERIALS

CARBON/ FIBERGLASS
• Most accurate
• Most consistent
• Very smooth
• Quiet

WOOD/ FIBERGLASS
• Accurate
• Consistent
• Very smooth
• Quietest

FIBERGLASS LAMINATE
• Accurate
• Consistent
• Not as smooth
• Noisier

SOLID FIBERGLASS
• Not as accurate
• Not as consistent
• Smooth
• Quiet

RISERS

DEFLEXED RISER
• Easiest to shoot accurately
• Most forgiving
• Slower arrow flight
• Quieter

STRAIGHT RISER
• Harder to shoot accurately
• Less forgiving
• Fast arrow flight
• Noisier

WHEELS

CAMS
• Fastest
• Hardest to shoot accurately
• Less smooth
• Noisier

ENERGY WHEELS
• Fast
• Easier to shoot accurately
• Smooth
• Quieter

STANDARD WHEELS
• Slower
• Easiest to shoot accurately
• Smoothest
• Quietest

SPEED vs. ACCURACY. Selecting the right bow always means a trade-off between speed and accuracy. A fast bow offers a flatter trajectory, but is less forgiving of minor inconsistencies in shooting form. Most beginners opt for accuracy over sheer speed; a fast bow requires considerably more practice to shoot consistently.

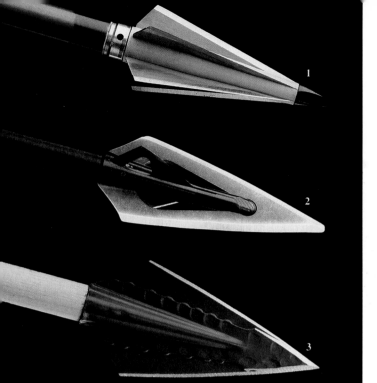

BROADHEAD STYLES include: (1) replaceable-blade type, in which the blades or entire cartridge (opposite page) is changed when the blades become dull; (2) center-insert type, in which only the center blade is replaced; and (3) nonreplaceable type, whose blades can be resharpened.

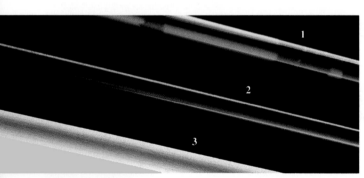

SHAFT TYPES include: (1) aluminum, which is consistent in quality, but may bend; (2) carbon, which costs more, but has a smaller diameter, penetrates deeper and can't be ruined by bending; (3) wood, which is least expensive, but may vary in weight, warp or break.

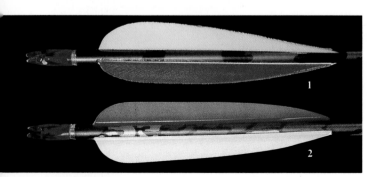

FLETCHING TYPES include: (1) feather, which provides good stability, especially on heavy arrows and (2) plastic, which is waterproof and durable.

Arrows

For consistent accuracy, all of your arrows must be straight and uniform. Shafts should be identical in length, weight and diameter, and made of material that won't warp, such as aluminum or carbon.

Once you've determined your draw length (p. 50), select arrows about an inch longer. If an arrow is too short, you may overdraw and the arrow will fall off the rest, possibly causing an injury. If you shoot arrows longer than necessary, the extra weight will affect velocity and trajectory.

Other important considerations when selecting arrows include shaft size, weight and stiffness.

Shaft size refers to the outside diameter and the wall thickness, which determine the weight of the shaft (measured in grains) and its stiffness, or *spine*. Large-diameter, thin-walled shafts are light, fast and have a flat trajectory. Small-diameter, thick-walled shafts are heavier and slower, but deliver more energy to the target.

If your arrows do not have the correct spine, they will fly erratically (p. 71). Refer to a shaft selection chart (opposite page) to determine the arrows that can be shot effectively from your bow.

Feather or plastic vanes, or *fletching*, help rotate and stabilize an arrow in flight, making it more accurate. The arrow's notched end, or *nock*, and the fletching should be brightly colored. This will help you follow the arrow in flight and locate it after the shot.

Broadheads come in many styles, weights and sizes. Check regulations to find out which are legal in your state. To ensure that the broadhead you select matches the spine of your arrow, consult an archery shop pro. Test several recommended styles to determine which your bow shoots most accurately.

Another consideration: broadheads should weigh and shoot about the same as the target points you use when practicing. Then, you won't have to make a major correction when hunting season arrives.

Broadheads must be razor sharp to achieve maximum penetration and slice blood vessels. On long hunts, carry replaceable blades or cartridges or sharpening tools.

REPLACE cartridge-style broadheads (top) by slipping the cartridge over the ferrule on the shaft, then screwing in the point. Sharpen nonreplaceable broadheads (bottom) with a mill file or special sharpening tools.

RELEASE arrows using: (1) a leather shooting glove, which protects your fingers; (2) a *tab*, which provides a smoother release; or (3) a mechanical release, which releases the string smoothly for the most accurate shots.

How to Interpret a Shaft Selection Chart

COMPOUND BOW Actual or Calculated Peak Bow Weight			CORRECT ARROW LENGTH – YOUR DRAW LENGTH PLUS 1" CLEARANCE												
			27"			28"			29"			30"			
Broadhead or Field Point Weight Only			(Shaft Characteristics)												
90-110 grain	115-135 grain	140-160 grain	Size	Model	Weight	Size	Model	Weight	Size	Model	Weight	Size	Model	Weight
56-61	53-58	50-55	2113	XX75	251 C	2213	XX75	275 A	2312	XX75	272 A	2312	XX75	282 B
			2114	XX75	266 B	2114	XX75	276 C	2213	XX75	285 B	2314	XX75	319 A
			2016	XX75	285 C	2115	XX75	302 B	2215	XX75	309 A	2215	XX75	320 B
			2115	XX75	291 A	2018	XX75	344 B	2117	XX75	349 A	2117	XX75	361 B
			2018	XX75	332 A	2020	XX75	378 A	2020	XX75	391 B	2216	XX75	361 A
62-67	59-64	56-61	2213	XX75	265 A	2312	XX75	263 A	2312	XX75	272 B	2413	XX75	312 A
			2114	XX75	266 C	2213	XX75	275 B	2314	XX75	309 A	2314	XX75	319 B
			2115	XX75	291 B	2215	XX75	299 A	2215	XX75	309 B	2315	XX75	350 A
			2018	XX75	332 B	2117	XX75	337 A	2117	XX75	349 B	2216	XX75	361 B
			2020	XX75	364 A	2020	XX75	378 B	2216	XX75	349 A	2219	XX75	413 A
68-73	65-70	62-67	2312	XX75	254 A	2312	XX75	263 B	2413	XX75	302 A	2512	XX75	305 A
			2213	XX75	265 B	2314	XX75	298 A	2314	XX75	309 B	2413	XX75	312 B
			2215	XX75	288 A	2215	XX75	299 B	2315	XX75	338 A	2315	XX75	350 B
			2117	XX75	325 A	2117	XX75	337 B	2216	XX75	349 B	2219	XX75	413 B
			2020	XX75	364 B	2216	XX75	337 A	2219	XX75	399 A			

SELECT the correct arrow using a shaft selection chart in an arrow catalog (this excerpt shows only how to select arrows for compounds, but the charts also include information for recurves). First, locate the box that includes your bow weight (most catalogs provide instructions for determining calculated peak bow weight for compounds). Look in the column that shows the weight of your broadheads. Next, move across that row to the box beneath your correct arrow length. You can use any shaft listed in the box, but the ones in bold type are used most commonly.

Clothing

Clothes for deer hunting should keep you quiet, safe, and comfortable, yet well hidden. Be sure to choose clothing that suits the weather and your hunting style, and conforms to all regulations.

OUTERWEAR. Wear soft, quiet outerwear made of wool, fleece or cotton. Hard-finish fabrics rustle and swish as you move or brush against branches, making it tough for you to hear whitetails and easy for them to hear you.

Most states require blaze, or "hunter" orange, outerwear during firearms, but not archery-only, deer seasons. Check regulations to determine minimum amounts. The bright color helps other hunters see you. Though you may also be more visible to deer, they're more likely to notice motion than color.

While the safest outerwear is solid blaze orange, a camouflage version with dark blotches makes you less noticeable to deer. But it also makes you less obvious to other hunters, so it's not legal everywhere.

Some hunters wear a complete outfit of blaze orange while walking to their stands, then strip down to the legal minimum, such as a blaze-orange cap and vest.

For bowhunting, choose camouflage colors and patterns that mimic your surroundings. In a given area, you may want green for early season, brown or gray later, and white for snow.

Clothing treated with an ultraviolet blocking agent supposedly lessens the chances of deer

Reversible coveralls can be used for gun or bowhunting

spotting you, but the effectiveness of such products has not been thoroughly tested.

INNER LAYERS. Layers of clothing under an outer shell retain more body heat and allow moisture to escape better than a single, heavy garment. Layering

BLAZE-ORANGE CAMO helps break up the solid-orange color and makes it more difficult for deer to see you. But this type of camo is also harder for humans to see, so it's a poor choice if there are other hunters around.

Camo Commonly Used for Bowhunting

LEAF CAMO blends in with leaves and branches. Some patterns are designed for coniferous forests.

TREE CAMO, patterned after real tree bark, works especially well for those who commonly hunt from tree stands.

SNOW CAMO is ideal in snow-covered woods or fields. It also blends well with the sky when stand-hunting.

MIXED CAMO, two colors or patterns, breaks up your outline better than a complete outfit of the same color.

also helps you cope with changing weather conditions. Carry extra clothes or zip-out linings in a daypack so you can shed or add layers as needed.

Wool is the traditional choice for inner layers because it maintains most of its insulation value when wet. Synthetic fleece is another good choice, with the same qualities as wool, at a lighter weight.

Clothing insulated with down is warmest, but retains little heat when wet and dries slowly. Clothing with synthetic insulation, such as Thinsulate and Hollofil, is nearly as warm, retains more heat when wet, yet dries quickly.

Polypropylene underwear wicks moisture away from the skin into the next layer of clothing, so you stay dryer and warmer. Cotton underwear, though popular, is a poor choice because it retains moisture.

Most raingear is noisy in the woods; if you need it, wear it under your quiet, outer layer.

FOOTWEAR. Whitetail hunters use a wide variety of leather and rubber boots, but those with rubber bottoms and leather uppers are the most versatile. Often called "pacs," these boots are light and leave less human scent than all-leather boots. They keep your feet dry when the ground is wet, yet the leather uppers allow your feet to breathe. If you don't like pacs, select boots with breathable, waterproof Gore-Tex liners.

Soft, flexible rubber or crepe soles allow you to feel objects underfoot. Vibram soles afford better traction in rough terrain, but don't allow you to feel what's underfoot as well. So you're more likely to snap twigs and make other noise when you walk.

Boots with Thinsulate insulation are ideal for cool weather. For cold weather, use pacs with removable felt liners. Cold-weather boots should be one size larger than normal so you can wear two heavy wool socks over a thin polypropylene sock. When hunting wetlands, even those that are frozen, wear hip boots or waders. The ice on a frozen marsh is seldom safe, especially in areas of emergent vegetation.

CAPS AND GLOVES. In warm weather, wear a lightweight Gore-Tex cap that keeps you dry, allows heat to escape and keeps the sun off your face. In cold weather, wear an insulated cap with earflaps. You may need a face mask in the coldest weather. Hoods, though warm, restrict peripheral vision and hearing.

Light leather gloves, such as golf gloves, work well in cool weather or in areas with lots of briars. Fingerless wool gloves are the best choice in colder weather. In very cold weather, switch to heavy mittens. Attach them to a thong draped around your neck so they drop conveniently at your side when you take them off for a shot. Some hunters prefer hand muffs to gloves or mittens.

Accessories

Travel light with a pack containing only the hunting accessories you really need. Don't load yourself down with gadgets.

PACKS. Fanny packs are best for carrying small amounts of gear. Because they fit snugly around your waist, they don't restrict arm movement or tire your shoulder and neck muscles.

Daypacks carry more gear. For comfort, select one with wide shoulder straps. Most packs are made of nylon, which is tough and water-repellent, but noisier than cotton, fleece or wool. Packs with small outside pockets are handy for carrying small items. Always use blaze-orange packs during the firearms deer season.

OPTICS. High-quality binoculars and spotting scopes give you bright, sharp images, making it easier to see deer in dim light or deep shadow.

Compact, rubber-coated binoculars are ideal for spotting deer, judging antlers and verifying your target. All binoculars are rated according to magnification and diameter of the objective lenses. A designation of 8 × 40, for instance, means that the binoculars magnify an object 8 times and have 40 mm objective lenses. Most whitetail hunters prefer binoculars in the 7x to 10x magnification range, but the higher the magnification, the narrower the field of view. Assuming the optics are of equal quality, large-diameter objective lenses gather more light than small ones.

Some hunters use spotting scopes to study whitetails at a distance. Variable-power scopes, about 20-45x, are also handy for checking targets at the range. Always support your spotting scope on a tripod or window mount.

Don't make the mistake of buying cheap binoculars and spotting scopes. Those with high-quality lenses and prisms give you much greater clarity and light-gathering capability. Consult an expert to make sure you buy optics that fit your needs.

COMPASS. Always carry a good compass and know how to use it. Many hunters carry a spare in their pack. Hold the compass away from your gun barrel or other metal objects to avoid false readings.

KNIVES, SAWS, AND SHEARS. You'll need a strong, sharp knife for field-dressing deer and doing other chores. Folding, lock-back knives with 3- to 5-inch blades are ideal. For gutting, skinning and caping, use blunt-nosed blades so you don't puncture the deer's intestines or cut through the hide.

Carry a saw, axe or machete to clear small trees and large branches from shooting lanes or areas around stands; use pruning shears to snip small branches. The most convenient saws are folding, lock-back models with hollow, threaded handles into which you can insert a long sapling to reach high limbs.

STOOLS AND CUSHIONS. Lightweight, folding stools with canvas or nylon seats are easy to carry and make you more comfortable on stand. Several models double as packs, with carrying straps and side pockets. A 5-gallon bucket also makes a handy stool and has plenty of room for lunch, a thermos and extra clothing. Cushions keep your rear dry, warm and protected from sharp rocks and branches. Select a cushion made of soft, quiet material that won't absorb water. It should fasten to your belt for easy carrying.

SCENTS. Two types are available: attractant scents and masking scents. Attractants contain urine, usually from a doe. Masking scents contain a wide variety of substances intented to cover human odor (p. 110).

The value of scents is a controversial topic. There have been no scientific studies to prove or disprove the merit of scents, but many accomplished hunters will attest to their effectiveness.

DAYPACK contents include: (1) raingear, (2) flashlight, (3) water bottle, (4) extra pair of socks, (5) camera, (6) binoculars, (7) knife, (8) pruning shears, (9) folding saw, (10) first-aid kit, (11) disposable handwarmer, (12) map of hunting area, (13) candle, (14) whistle, (15) waterproof matches, (16) compass, (17) lunch, (18) rubber gloves for field-dressing, (19) plastic bags for heart and liver, (20) pull-up rope, (21) extra boot laces, (22) drag rope, (23) attractant scent, (24) masking scent, (25) urine bottle and (26) toilet paper.

Preparing for
the Hunt

Landowners can give you specifics on where deer are commonly seen

Gathering Information

What happens in the split-second it takes to fire a shot is the subject of many deer-hunting stories. But most successful hunts begin much earlier, sometimes more than a year in advance. To make the best use of your time afield and improve your odds of shooting a deer, it pays to gather information and make your plans long before the season begins.

WHERE TO GO. For general advice on where to hunt, consult wildlife managers and conservation officers. While they may not reveal specific hunting spots, they can inform you about areas with high whitetail populations. For more specifics, talk to landowners, clerks at sporting goods stores, taxidermists, farmers, loggers, rural mail carriers or others who work in whitetail country.

By spring, wildlife managers usually have data on deer density, condition of the herd and harvest from the previous season. Managers may also know of areas where whitetails are damaging crops, Christmas trees, nursery stock or fruit trees. Landowners with

such problems will probably give you permission to hunt.

SPECIAL HUNTS. You may miss some great opportunities if you hunt only during the regular firearms deer season.

You can take advantage of archery and muzzleloader hunts, antlerless seasons and hunts held in areas overpopulated with deer. Ask conservation agencies about special hunts and how to apply for them.

Getting an early start is especially important when planning a hunt in another state or province. Become familiar with their regulations; they may differ greatly from those around home. For example, some states won't issue a nonresident license to anyone without a firearms-safety or hunter-education certificate, and getting one could take months.

MAPS. The following maps will help you find good hunting spots and plan your strategy afield:

County highway maps, available at highway department offices or county courthouses, show state, county and township roads.

Maps of state forests, wildlife management areas, national and provincial forests, wildlife refuges and waterfowl production areas are available from state, federal and provincial natural resource agencies.

Plat books, available at courthouses, list landowners and show property boundaries – valuable information for obtaining permission to hunt on private land.

County maps show even dirt and gravel roads

Topo maps show you the "lay of the land"

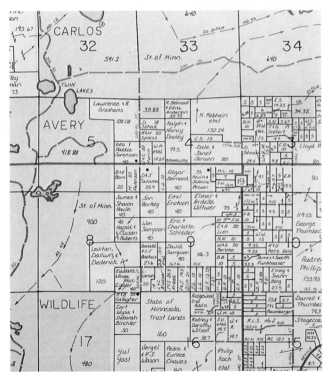

Plat books detail property lines

U.S. Geological Survey (USGS) topographic maps, often called "quads" or "topo" maps, are available from USGS offices and local map stores. Drawn from aerial photos, the maps have contour lines representing hills, valleys and other relief. They also show features such as roads, trails, wetlands, lakes, open fields and timber. The type most useful to hunters

has a 1:2,400 scale and covers about 50 square miles per sheet.

Aerial photos showing one square mile each are available from the county offices of the Agricultural Stabilization and Conservation Service (ASCS). They reveal considerably more detail than quads and are updated much more frequently. Stereoscopic photos allow three-dimensional viewing of topography, but they're not updated as often and require a stereoscope to read.

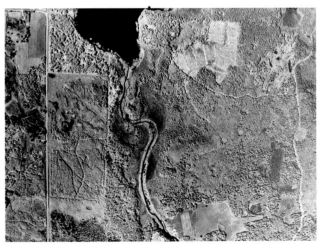

Aerial photos provide exact detail

Local chambers of commerce can provide maps of local trails and canoe routes that may give you access to good deer-hunting areas; they can also help you find accommodations.

Tracks give you an idea of how many deer are using an area and how often

Common Types of Deer Sign

BROWSING SIGN from deer and rabbits differs. Deer lack upper front teeth, so they tear off a bud, leaving a ragged end (top). A rabbit nips the twig off cleanly (bottom).

DROPPINGS from deer (top) are elongated and usually tightly grouped. Fresh ones are moist and soft. Rabbit droppings (bottom) are round and scattered more loosely.

TRAILS are made by deer traveling between cover and food. Follow a trail both ways to determine where the deer are coming from and where they are going.

Scouting

Accomplished deer hunters spend more time scouting than hunting. By the time they step into the woods, they know the habits of the deer and the best places to hunt.

Whether you're trying an area for the first time or hunting a familiar spot, scouting will improve your chances. Before scouting on private land, get permission from the landowner, who may help by telling you where deer have been seen.

GETTING STARTED. Become familiar with the cover and terrain in your hunting area, especially where you find the most deer sign. This will help you predict deer movements and determine which hunting techniques will work best.

Scout an area small enough to know intimately but large enough to contain the home ranges (p. 15) of several deer. Ambitious hunters might scout several square miles, even where deer densities are high, just because they enjoy it. Others might find heavy deer sign and familiarize themselves with only a small area, which is much easier to learn.

If you have time, scout several areas so you can "rest" one spot after a few days of hunting and move to another. It's always better, however, to scout one or two areas well than to scout several poorly.

SIGN. While you familiarize yourself with the terrain, look for trails, tracks, droppings, rubs and scrapes. Pay special attention to *funnels*, areas where topography, cover or man-made obstacles restrict movement of deer to a narrow corridor. In farm country, hair lodged in barbed-wire fences shows you where deer routinely cross.

Don't confine your scouting to well-worn trails; make side trips into likely looking cover. If you spot a deer, watch it and learn as much as possible about its movement pattern. Record important observations on a map (p. 65).

BEDS in cover (shown) signify a daytime bedding site; beds in fields or open areas, a nighttime site. A trail leading to a daytime bedding site makes a good stand location.

SHEDS are usually found in the spring in the area where a buck wintered. Next to seeing the deer, sheds are the best proof that a certain buck made it through the hunting season.

RUBS are the most important sign left by bucks before they start making scrapes. As a general rule, the larger the rub tree, the bigger the buck that made the rub.

ACTIVE SCRAPES mean a buck is using the area. A buck usually *freshens* an active scrape each day by pawing the bare soil to loosen the dirt and then rub-urinating on it (p. 31).

WHEN TO SCOUT. It pays to scout before, during and after the season. Over time, you'll learn the seasonal patterns of deer.

Archers should start scouting during late summer. The weather is still warm, so deer will be in shaded, cooler areas such as wetlands, mature timber or conifer stands. Look for fresh grazing sign on unharvested crops, grain residue, fruits and nut crops, especially acorns. Active feeding areas will have lots of fresh tracks and droppings. Where water is scarce, look for tracks around any water source.

For a reliable indication of rutting activity, firearms hunters should scout just before the season begins, after bucks start making rubs and scrapes.

To determine deer numbers and size of bucks, glass open feeding locations from a distant, elevated position before the season opens. In timber, you'll have to go into the woods to see deer. Observe as often as possible, then choose stands that allow you to intercept deer moving to feeding sites in the evening and back to cover in the morning. Seeing numerous deer while scouting also gives you the confidence to keep hunting all season.

Deer change their habits over the course of a long season. Or another hunter may take the animal you had your eye on. Scouting during the season will help you locate places where deer are currently most abundant.

To scout during the season without losing valuable hunting time, combine still-hunting and scouting. Still-hunting's slow pace leaves you plenty of time to study sign and learn new terrain.

Late in the season, after the rut is over, bucks feed more often and seek shelter from cold weather. Look for fresh signs of browsing. Concentrate your efforts in areas sheltered from the wind, such as thick conifer or mixed conifer-hardwood stands, swamps, south-facing slopes and brushy gullies, draws and ravines.

Postseason scouting enables you to gather some information that would have been difficult to get during the season. You can closely inspect rubs, scrapes and trails without having to worry about spooking deer or causing them to alter their patterns. Chances are, the sign will be in about the same location next year.

Combining a hunt for cast or shed antlers with postseason scouting is becoming increasingly popular with serious whitetail hunters. "Sheds" not only make great trophies, but are positive proof that a buck made it through the hunting season. And there's a good chance he will grow an even bigger rack next year.

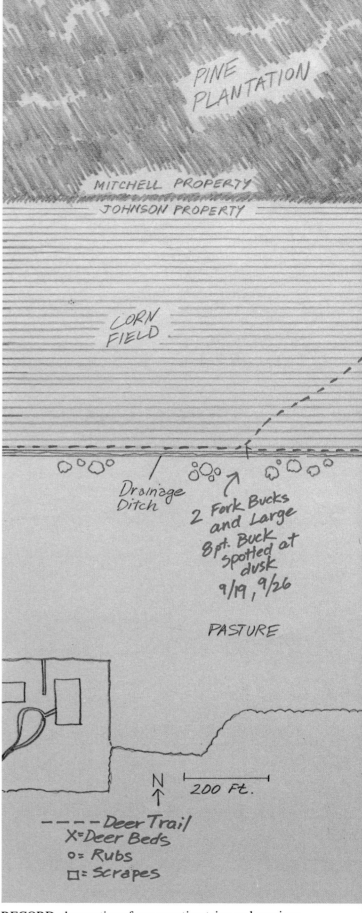

RECORD observations from scouting trips and previous hunts on a hand-drawn map of your hunting area. Sketch in roads, buildings, features of the terrain, habitat types

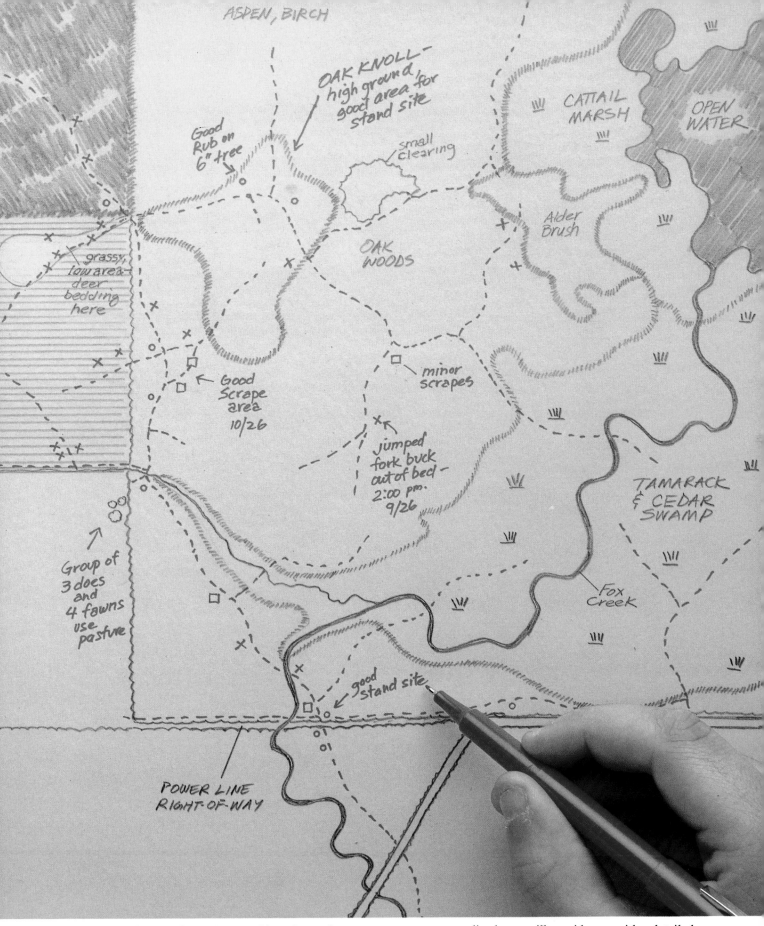

ASPEN, BIRCH

OAK KNOLL — high ground, good area for stand site

Good Rub on 6" tree

small clearing

CATTAIL MARSH

OPEN WATER

Alder Brush

OAK WOODS

grassy, low area— deer bedding here

Good Scrape area 10/26

minor scrapes

jumped fork buck out of bed — 2:00 p.m. 9/26

TAMARACK & CEDAR SWAMP

Group of 3 does and 4 fawns use pasture

Fox Creek

good stand site

POWER LINE RIGHT-OF-WAY

and property lines. Indicate dates and locations of scrapes and rubs, and where you found beds, deer trails and sheds. Also note any actual deer sightings. In time,

your personalized map will provide you with a detailed account of how the deer are using the area and will help you decide on the best places to hunt.

Sighting In Firearms

Just because your gun shot perfectly last season is no assurance it will do so this year. A sharp blow, warped stock or loose scope mounts can make you miss a deer. Serious deer hunters sight in before every season.

You'll also have to sight in any new firearms or those with new sights. If you're using a gun that someone else sighted in, take it to the target range and make sure it shoots accurately for you too; each hunter sees sights a bit differently.

All firearms, including rifles, muzzleloaders, shotguns with slugs and handguns should be carefully sighted in.

Sight in well before the season, taking advantage of calm, sunny weather. Bullet drift will be minimal and it will be easy to see your targets and work with small tools to adjust your sights.

Most target ranges offer shooting benches, target stands and solid backstops. Ask permission before sighting in on private land. Before using public land, make sure target shooting is legal.

Equipment for sighting in includes sandbags or other gun rests, ear protectors, targets, sight-adjusting tools such as screwdrivers or hex keys, and tape for covering bullet holes in the target before shooting again. A spotting scope enables you to see bullet holes from your shooting position.

Sight in using the exact ammunition you will use for hunting. Different loads and bullet weights may result in different trajectories. Even seemingly identical cartridges loaded by different companies may not shoot the same in your rifle.

To steady your gun and minimize human error, cradle it on sandbags or some other soft but stable rest. Relax, hold the gun firmly with your cheek squarely on the stock, and take a few deep breaths. Exhale halfway, hold your breath and gently squeeze the trigger.

To check a rifle, muzzleloader or slug gun that shot well last year, fire a 3-shot group from 100 yards to make sure the sights haven't changed. To sight in new firearms, those with new sights, shotguns without sights, handguns or any gun you suspect is not sighted in, shoot at a target 25 yards away.

If you miss at 25 yards, "bore-sight" the gun to save ammunition. With a bolt action, remove the bolt, look through the receiver end of the barrel, center the bullseye in the bore and secure the firearm so it can't move. Adjust your sights to aim at the bullseye. Replace the bolt, fire a shot and continue to adjust the sights until you're satisfied. If your action does not allow a direct look through the bore, you'll need a bore-sighting tool.

Move the target farther away to make fine adjustments – 100 yards for muzzleloaders, rifles and slug guns; 50 yards for pistols and shotguns without sights. Then fire 3 shots and note the location of the center of the group. If you're not on target, adjust the sights and continue firing 3-shot groups until you're satisfied with the accuracy.

To adjust iron sights, move the rear sight in the direction you want the point of impact to move. Raise it to make the gun shoot higher; move it to the left to shoot farther left.

To adjust scopes, turn the horizontal and vertical adjuster screws in the direction indicated by arrows near the screw heads.

With a flat-shooting rifle, adjust the sights to hit 2 to 3 inches high at 100 yards. This way, you'll be dead-on at 200 yards and only slightly low at 300 yards. A ballistics table will tell you how much your bullet will drop. Be sure to fire several 3-shot groups at 200 and 300 yards to check long-range accuracy.

A good rifle in the hands of an expert marksman will put three shots in a 1-inch circle at 100 yards.

If you drop your gun during the hunt, fire a shot to make sure it's still sighted in.

Tips for Sighting In

ADJUST your scope by turning the horizontal or vertical adjuster screws. On most scopes, one click will move the point of impact ¼ inch at 100 yards. Refer to your scope manual for complete adjustment instructions.

COVER each 3-shot group with tape before making adjustments and firing another group. This will prevent you from becoming confused by too many bullet holes in the same target.

SIGHT IN with the same load you use for hunting. Different-weight bullets of the same caliber usually don't impact in the same spot, as shown here with a 3-shot group using 120-grain bullets and one using 180-grain bullets.

Shooting Firearms

After sighting in, try shooting targets in the field under realistic hunting conditions. Shoot from a variety of positions, slopes and distances, and under different wind and light conditions. This will improve your marksmanship and can make the difference between a near miss and a clean kill.

Before practicing, check regulations on preseason shooting. In some states, it's against the law to take firearms legal for deer into the field right before the deer season.

Rules of safety are as important in field-shooting practice as in hunting. Select an area away from people, livestock, roads and buildings: Place targets in front of backstops such as embankments or trees. Always look beyond your target before firing.

To improve your accuracy under various hunting conditions, practice shooting from each of the positions shown below. Practice without a rest, but when hunt-ing, use a solid rest if you can. Place your hand or arm between the gun and the rest; resting the gun directly on a hard object will cause it to shoot errati-cally. You're ready to shoot deer when you can put 90 percent of your shots in an 8-inch paper plate at the distance you plan to shoot.

Shooting conditions in the field are seldom ideal. You must learn to cope with a variety of problems. Crosswinds, for instance, blow bullets off course. A 30-m.p.h. wind blowing at right angles to the path of a 150-grain .30-06 bullet will cause it to drift 10 inches at 200 yards. Compensate by aiming upwind.

Shooting uphill or downhill causes bullets to hit high, a phenomenon called *slant-range effect*. The reason: firearms are sighted in to compensate for the drop in a bullet's flight caused by the vertical pull of gravity. This drop is greatest when the bullet's path is horizontal. The closer the bullet's path to vertical, the higher above the line of sight it will hit. A 150-grain .30-06 bullet shot at a 60-degree angle <u>uphill or downhill</u> will hit 4½ inches above the line of sight at a range of 200 yards.

Practice shooting on steep slopes or from an elevated stand to determine how low you have to aim to compensate for the slant-range effect.

Common Shooting Positions (instructions for right-hander)

PRONE. With your body about 30 degrees left of your line of aim, place your left elbow just left of the rifle. Pull your right leg forward to lift your stomach. The prone posi-tion is the most accurate, but brush and other obstructions may preclude ground-level shooting.

SITTING. With your legs about 30 degrees right of your line of aim, rest both elbows firmly on your knees, avoid-ing bone-to-bone contact. This is the best position if vegetation, rocks or the terrain prevent you from using the prone position.

You may have to compensate even more on downhill targets; they often look farther away than they really are, so the tendency is to aim higher.

Unless you're proficient on moving targets, don't shoot at running deer; the risk of only wounding the animal is too great. Go to a shooting range that has moving, life-size targets. Or shoot at targets placed inside old tires and rolled down a hill. Your lead will depend on caliber, bullet weight and distance. With a 150-grain .30-06 bullet, for instance, a crossing shot at 100 yards requires a 4- to 5-foot lead. At 300 yards, the lead increases to 15 to 20 feet. You're ready to shoot running deer when you can consistently hit an 8-inch circle at the distance you plan to shoot.

Another way to hone your shooting skills: try hunting small game with a .22 rimfire, or varmints with your deer rifle. If you use lighter bullets for varmints, remember to sight in with your regular hunting load before deer season.

It's always easier to hit a practice target than a real deer. As a deer approaches, move your gun into shooting position when the deer passes behind cover. Don't look at the rack, eyes, tail or whole deer; concentrate only on the precise spot you wish to hit. Shoot when the deer pauses or steps into an opening.

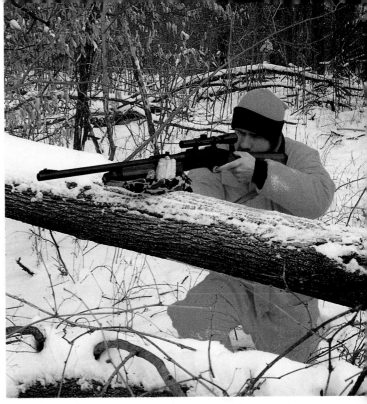

SOLID REST. Whenever possible, find a solid rest for your gun, regardless of shooting position. Place your hand, arm, hat, pack or other pliable object between the forearm and the rest. Otherwise, the gun bounces from the recoil, throwing your shot off target.

KNEELING. With your body 45 degrees left of the line of aim, sit on your right foot. Keep your left foot forward and brace your left elbow on the knee. The kneeling position is steadier than the offhand, not as steady as the sitting position.

OFFHAND. With feet parallel to the line of aim, spread your legs to shoulder width and keep your left elbow close to your body. A sling will help steady your aim. The offhand position is the toughest to master. Practice it in case you have to make a quick shot.

Tuning & Shooting a Bow

Shooting an arrow accurately enough to bag a whitetail requires consistent form, diligent practice, and a bow that's been properly tuned and sighted in.

The best archers may differ in form, but the way they hold the bow, draw it and release the arrow remains consistent from shot to shot. Practice your form while a friend watches from the side and back for consistency.

Archery ranges, indoor and outdoor, are the safest places to practice. Indoor shooting leagues allow you to enjoy the sport all year. Backyard ranges are the most convenient, but make sure they're legal and safe. Erect a backstop, such as a wall of straw bales, to stop your arrows.

Practice with target points. Begin shooting at a target 10 yards away. To adjust the sights, move the sight pin in the direction of your error. If

Set sight pins for distances at which you most commonly shoot

BEND at the waist when shooting down from a tree stand. If you drop your bow arm instead, the tendency is to change your anchor point, causing you to shoot erratically. Once you decide to shoot at the deer, do not look at the whole deer; concentrate only on the precise spot you want the arrow to hit.

you're shooting low, for instance, lower the sight pin. If you're shooting to the right, move the pin to the right. To extend your range, practice until you can consistently hit a plate-size target at 20 yards; continue extending your range in 5-yard increments.

If your accuracy does not seem to be improving after a few practice sessions, look for one of the following problems:

· The bow may be too powerful, causing you to shake when you release the arrow.

· You may be shooting an arrow with the wrong spine. Too little spine causes an arrow to veer right; too much, left. Size and weight also make a difference. Consult an arrow-selection chart (p. 53).

· If you use a tab or glove, you may be "pulling off" – pulling your hand away from your face as you release the arrow.

· Some very fast compound bows are "temperamental" and difficult to shoot accurately without a mechanical release.

· You may not be pulling the string to the same anchor point with each shot; your draw length will be inconsistent and so will your shots.

· The bow may not be properly tuned. From a distance of 6 feet, shoot an arrow through paper stretched over a frame. The pattern left by the fletching should have a uniform triangular shape. If the bow is out of tune, the arrow will fishtail (wobble from side to side) or porpoise (undulate up and down), resulting in a pattern wider or longer than normal.

An arrow from a properly tuned bow will leave a hole like this

An arrow that does not fly true loses velocity and penetration. Take your bow to an archery shop for the necessary adjustments. Fast bows are most difficult to tune. A bow will remain tuned unless you change such things as the draw weight, anchor point or arrow model.

Once you've sighted in and your arrows are flying well, practice in the field. Wear hunting clothes to make sure they don't interfere with your shooting.

Before going hunting, remember to practice with broadheads; they may fly a little differently than target points. Don't shoot broadheads into conventional targets, because they're difficult to pull out. Shoot at a paper or cardboard target in front of a dirt pile.

PRACTICE by standing crossways to the target with your feet shoulder-width apart. Place most of your weight on your front foot. Keep your bow hand relaxed and the back of your draw hand straight; be sure to draw to a consistent anchor point. Release the string and hold the bow steady until the arrow strikes.

Practice in strong winds to determine the effects of wind drift. Slant-range effect (p. 68) is not important at the distances archers normally shoot.

Shoot while sitting and standing in tree stands. Always use a safety belt to prevent falling and to brace against while making shots at awkward angles. For best accuracy while shooting downward, bend at the waist instead of dropping your bow arm.

Many excellent bowhunters consider "stump-shooting" the best practice for hunting. Stump-shooters walk through uninhabited woods or fields, taking shots at targets such as stumps and logs. Practice shooting while crouched, kneeling and standing, preferably in cover. Learn to gauge distance by pacing off the yardage after each shot. Use judo points to avoid losing arrows.

Judo points are best for stump-shooting

VITAL AREAS on a whitetail include: (1) brain, (2) spinal column, (3) jugular vein, (4) lung, (5) heart and (6) liver. A deer hit in any of these locations will not go far, and you should be able to recover it. However, only the heart-lung area provides a large target and a comfortable margin of error. If you shoot too high, you'll hit the spine; too far forward, the base of the neck; and too far to the rear, the liver.

Shot Placement

With a little luck, you may get one or two "perfect" shots in a lifetime. Ideally, the animal would be in the open, and standing broadside at close range. But more often, you'll have to shoot while the deer is partially screened by vegetation, moving, or at a less-than-ideal angle.

Regardless of the circumstances, the best bet is to aim for the heart-lung area. On a mature whitetail, this area is about the size of a paper plate. It's the biggest target of all whitetail vital areas. And even if you're a little off-target, you'll probably kill the deer anyway (see above).

Some veteran whitetail hunters swear by the neck shot, but it's much riskier than the heart-lung shot. The spinal column and jugular vein make up less than 25 percent of the neck's total area. A hit anywhere else in the neck will only wound the deer.

Trying to break the deer's back is equally risky. Shoot high and you miss the deer completely; low and you may only wound it. A brain shot will drop the deer instantly, but the brain is a very small target, and a deer is often moving its head even when standing still.

Even the heart-lung area may be difficult to hit, especially if the deer is walking toward you or away from you, or if you're shooting down at a sharp angle. Study the photos on these pages so you'll know where to place your shot regardless of your shooting angle or which way the deer is facing.

Ground-Level Shots

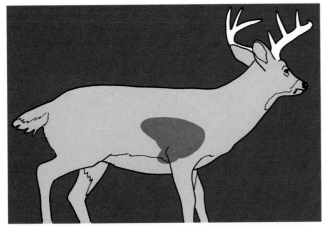

BROADSIDE. With 100 percent of the heart-lung area exposed, you have a target roughly the size of an 8-inch paper plate, with additional room for error.

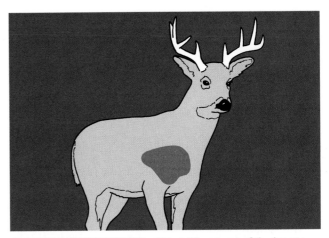

QUARTERING TOWARD. About 65 percent of the heart-lung area is exposed. Aim for the near shoulder. Don't try this shot with a bow; you'll hit the shoulder bone.

QUARTERING AWAY. About 60 percent of the heart-lung area is exposed. To hit the vitals, aim along an imaginary line through the deer's far shoulder.

HEAD-ON. With only 35 percent of the heart-lung area exposed, this shot is too risky for archers. Gun hunters should take it only if the deer is about to bolt.

Steep-Angle Shots

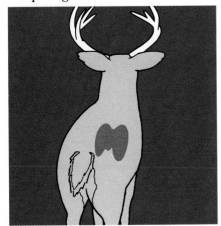

WALKING AWAY. About 45 percent of the heart-lung area is exposed. The tendency is to shoot too far forward; aim along an imaginary line exiting between the deer's front legs.

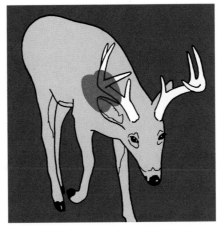

QUARTERING TOWARD. About 55 percent of the heart-lung area is exposed, but it is protected by the shoulder bone, and the deer will probably see you move as you prepare to shoot.

QUARTERING AWAY. About 55 percent of the heart-lung area is exposed. Aim along an imaginary line exiting low on the far shoulder. The deer is not likely to see your movement.

Safety

Statistics show that you're less likely to be injured while hunting than driving to your favorite spot. Decades of firearms-safety and hunter-education courses, and increased use of hunter-orange clothing have reduced shooting accidents. Nevertheless, every deer hunter must remember that firearms and bows can become lethal in a careless instant.

Make sure you and your companions take the following precautions:

· Keep guns, ammunition, bows and arrows away from kids. Lock up guns and ammo separately.

· Assume every gun is loaded. Check for cartridges in the magazine and chamber every time you pick up a gun.

· Don't aim at anything you don't intend to shoot. Assume a firearm may go off at any time, whether it's loaded or not. If you fall, keep the gun pointed away from yourself and others.

· Guard against accidental firing. Leave your safety on until just before you shoot. In situations where you might trip, such as crossing fences, creeks and ditches, unload your gun.

· Watch where you shoot. Never fire toward other hunters, buildings or livestock. Don't shoot over a road or ridge. A hard surface, such as frozen ground, ice, a rock or even water, can cause your bullet to ricochet.

· Carry only one caliber of ammunition. Accidentally firing the wrong cartridge in your gun can injure you and ruin your gun.

· Keep the barrel clear. Check your gun's barrel before you go afield; check again after a fall, because dirt or snow may plug it. Shooting with the barrel obstructed can cause it to bulge or burst and injure you.

· Protect yourself by protecting your broadheads. Sharp hunting points are dangerous. Use a quiver that completely covers the broadheads. Never walk or still-hunt with an arrow nocked.

· See and be seen. Wear blaze orange when deer hunting with firearms. Never do anything that could make someone mistake you for a deer, such as draping a deer over your shoulders to carry it out of the woods.

· Prepare for the unexpected. Anyone can get lost or hurt and end up in the woods longer than expected. Carry a good compass and other basic survival gear including a water bottle, snacks, waterproof matches, a flashlight and a whistle to summon help. Tell someone where you will be hunting and when you will return. A three-shot volley is the universal distress signal.

· Never drink alcohol before or during a hunt. Alcohol impairs your judgment and coordination and causes your body to lose heat faster than normal.

Visibility of Different Clothing Colors

COLOR of clothing makes a difference. Red (left) is the most difficult for other hunters to see. Blaze-orange camouflage (middle) shows up better than red, but is not as visible as solid blaze orange (right). Highly visible clothing is a must in heavily hunted areas. Check regulations to see which colors are legal where you hunt.

Safety Tips

NEVER SHOOT over hills or ridges, or when there are buildings or livestock in the background. A bullet from a high-power rifle can carry more than a mile.

UNLOAD your firearm when you return to your camp or vehicle; prop guns in a spot where they won't slip off. As a courtesy to other members of your party, leave the action open so they know your gun is unloaded.

RAISE and lower your unloaded gun or bow with a rope when hunting from an elevated stand. Make sure the barrel is pointing away from you. Always wear a safety belt while on stand to prevent a serious fall.

Verifying Your Target

CHECK any questionable form with binoculars. To the naked eye (left), a silhouette moving through the brush could easily be mistaken for a deer. But when viewed with binoculars (right), the form is not only magnified, it is much brighter. Then it becomes obvious that the form is that of a hunter ducking under branches.

Hunting Techniques

See Stalking (p. 92)

Stand-Hunting

When whitetails are on the move, stand-hunting is the easiest and most effective way to hunt them. The technique works best when the animals are most active – early and late in the day, during the rut and any time hunting pressure causes them to move more than they normally do.

A stand-hunter assumes a position where whitetails travel or have been active, and waits motionlessly until they move into shooting range. Successful stand-hunting requires proper timing, the right conditions, good stand locations and patience.

SELECTING STAND SITES. To locate the best stand sites, scout for rubs, active scrapes and fresh droppings and tracks.

Always select several stand sites so you can choose the best stand for the wind direction. If possible, select stands where you can see or hear deer before they're in range.

PREPARING YOUR STAND. A stand site may be ideal except that branches and brush interfere with your vision; they could also deflect a bullet or arrow and restrict movement of your gun or bow. To overcome these problems, clear your shooting lanes with a pruning shears or bow saw, but don't remove too much of your cover.

Archers usually cut lanes less than 30 yards long; gun hunters may extend them to 100 yards. Always ask permission before cutting on private land, and check regulations for cutting on public land.

When approaching your stand, avoid making unnecessary noise; don't walk on dry leaves or through thick brush. If a quiet approach is impossible, get to your stand earlier than normal.

Keep in mind that if you hunt far from a road, you'll need the equipment and endurance to drag your deer out of the woods.

CHANGING STANDS. Many hunters have what they consider a "lucky" stand, and they stick with it

Tips for Preparing Stand Sites

PRUNE limbs from nearby trees or tie back those in your tree to ensure a clear shot. Tying back the branches may help break up your outline.

REMOVE debris from the final approach to your stand, assuming you can walk in quietly most of the way. It's not practical to clear a long path.

SCRAPE away leaves and twigs from underfoot so you can move your feet silently when shifting position or preparing for a shot.

CLEAR your shooting lanes by cutting stems squarely and close to the ground. Otherwise, sharp edges can rip clothing and cause injuries.

no matter what. But you'll greatly improve your chances if you have several stands to choose from and pick the right one for the current weather conditions and time of day.

Wind direction is the first and most important consideration. Always select a stand downwind or crosswind of the location where you expect to see deer. This lessens the chances that the animals will smell you. If the wind switches during the day, move to another stand.

Wind velocity, though less important, provides some clues to good stand selection. If the wind is light, less than 10 m.p.h., take a stand near a trail, because deer are likely to be on the move. If the wind is stronger, take up a position in or near heavy cover, such as brush or cattails, where whitetails will likely hole up.

In hilly terrain, pick a site on high ground in the morning, because air currents that rise from the warming land will carry your scent upward, away from approaching deer. In the afternoon, as cooling air carries your scent downhill, select sites on lower ground.

During prerut, position your stand along a rub line (p. 29). After the rut begins, choose a stand overlooking an active scrape (p. 63).

If possible, pick a shady site to hide your silhouette and reduce glare from your face, glasses and gun – beacons advertising your location. If you're looking into the sun, you'll have a hard time seeing and shooting at deer. If you're backlit, however, deer will have difficulty seeing you.

When daytime temperatures are above freezing, choose midday stands near cover such as conifer stands, cattail sloughs and dense woodlots. A heavy winter coat combined with heat from digestion cause deer to seek "cooler" cover, even though temperatures may seem chilly to humans. During extremely cold weather, select stands near sunny areas protected from the wind. In arid climates, choose stands near watering holes.

How to Choose a Stand Site

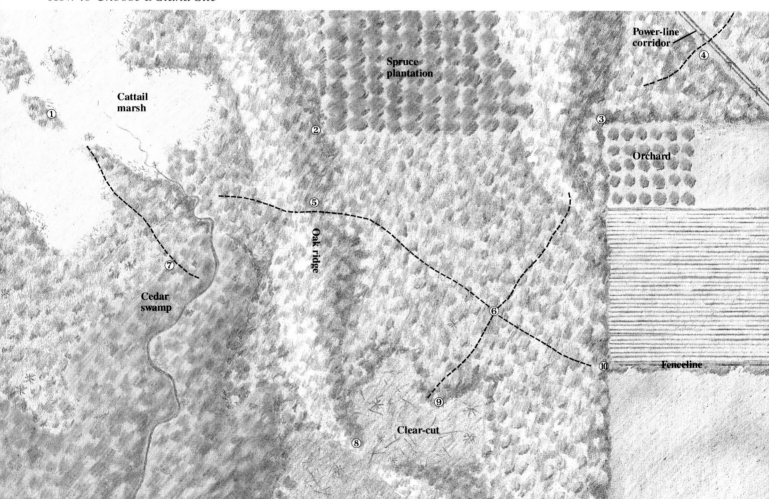

SELECT a stand (1) on one of several small islands in a cattail marsh, (2) where an oak ridge meets a spruce plantation, (3) in the corner of an orchard, (4) where a trail crosses a power-line corridor, (5) on a saddle on an oak ridge, (6) at a trail intersection, (7) where a trail enters a cedar swamp, (8) at the edge of a clear-cut between two oak ridges, (9) on a point jutting into a clear-cut and (10) at the junction of a fenceline and the woods.

In the morning, pick stands near wooded or brushy cover where deer are likely to bed; in the evening, near feeding areas or on trails leading to them. This pattern holds true during early archery seasons, before the gun season disrupts normal deer activity.

On opening day of the firearms season, deer often abandon trails used before the season and stay in thick cover to avoid hunters. Place your stand accordingly.

When a storm approaches, deer move around more, so it pays to take a stand near heavily used trails and feeding areas. After a major storm, deer may not resume normal activities for a day or two.

WHAT TO DO ON STAND. Even if there's a lot of sign around your stand, you may have to wait a long time to see a deer. If you're uncomfortable, it's difficult to sit still and stay alert. Make sure you have enough clothes and something to eat and drink. Sit on an insulated cushion to keep your rear warm and dry. Hold your firearm or bow rather than setting it down; this way, you'll always be ready to shoot.

Urinating on the ground near your stand may alert deer to your presence. Instead, use a plastic bottle with a screw-on cap or a hot-water bottle.

You must detect deer before they detect you. Listen carefully for rustling leaves and snapping twigs. You'll soon learn to differentiate between noises made by deer and those made by other animals, such as birds and squirrels.

If you hear sounds but can't see what made them, look from side to side, moving only your eyes. If you hear or see nothing more, turn your head as slowly as you can, first to one side and then the other. If you make any fast movements, the deer will probably see you.

If you spot a deer, try to read its signals. If it flicks its tail, it senses something is wrong, but has not identified the source of alarm. Remain still and wait for it to resume what it was doing. Even if the deer heard you, it may not spook if you don't move. However, if the deer lifts its tail to flagging position, it's ready to bolt. Fire if you have a clear shot.

Tips for Stand-Hunting

SCREW-IN STEPS (left) help you climb any tree. Folding models take up less room in your pack, but cost more than nonfolding models (shown). If you plan to use the tree again, remove the steps and put matchsticks or twigs in the holes (right) so you can easily find them next time.

PORTABLE LADDERS (left) are an alternative to screw-in steps. Most are made of aluminum and measure 12 to 14 feet in length. They break into 3- to 4-foot sections (right), strap securely to the tree and come with carrying straps for easy backpacking.

RANGE MARKERS are especially important to archers who use sights. Place bits of toilet paper on bushes at distances corresponding to those of your sight pins. This way, when a deer approaches one of your markers, you'll know which sight pin to use.

REFLECTIVE TACKS or reflective adhesive strips applied to trees beforehand make it easy to find your stand in the dark. Before moving to a new stand, be sure to remove the tacks so you don't clutter the woods and confuse other hunters.

81

STRAP-ON STANDS are easy to put up and will work on any tree. Adjustable straps or chains hold them in place. Use tree steps or a portable ladder to climb the tree.

Types of Stands

Most stand-hunting is done from elevated stands, but some hunters build ground blinds or simply sit against a tree or stump.

ELEVATED STANDS. Elevated stands make it easy for you to see deer but difficult for deer to see and smell you.

From an elevated stand you can spot deer at a distance and prepare for a shot while remaining above their normal line of sight. Much of your scent floats above any downwind deer or dissipates before it reaches the ground.

Although elevated stands conceal you, they don't make you invisible. You still must remain motionless to avoid attracting attention and spooking deer.

SELF-CLIMBING STANDS can be used only on trees with no branches below the desired stand height. They eliminate the need for tree steps or ladders, but they're physically demanding to use.

PERMANENT TREE STANDS offer the most comfort, but require frequent maintenance to keep them safe. Deer become accustomed to such stands once they have weathered and the new-wood smell disappears.

A tree limb is the oldest type of elevated stand, but it's also the least comfortable. If the tree is dead, or has dead overhead limbs, it could be dangerous, especially in windy weather. Always pick a tree big enough so the leaves and branches don't move when you shift your weight.

Portable stands keep you comfortable, so you're more likely to sit still. They include strap-on, self-climbing and ladder models. Portable tripod stands work well in areas with few trees. Many hunters put up several portable stands to make moving between sites easier.

Hunters commonly erect permanent elevated stands along traditional deer routes, and use them year after year. However an immovable stand is worthless if the wind direction is wrong, or deer have changed their movement pattern.

Check regulations before using an elevated stand. Some states have height restrictions, others allow only stands that will not damage trees and a few prohibit any kind of elevated stand. Permanent stands are illegal on most public lands.

GROUND STANDS AND BLINDS. Deadfalls, clumps of brush, tree trunks, rocks, stone walls or any other object that breaks up your outline makes a good ground stand. You can simply stand or sit on the ground, but a strap-on or screw-in tree seat or folding stool makes you more comfortable.

To conceal yourself more thoroughly, construct a ground blind from brush and logs. Or drape camouflage cloth over some sturdy branches, which double as a rest for your gun. The blind should be high enough to thoroughly conceal you while you're sitting on a stool.

Pit blinds are sometimes used on wide-open western prairies and flat midwestern farmlands, where whitetails live in areas nearly devoid of cover. Although they keep you well concealed, digging them is back-breaking work.

A 3-foot pit with a fringe of grass or brush provides thorough concealment. Mark the pit well when it's not in use, and fill it in after the season so people don't drive or fall into it.

To keep warm and dry, some hunters use small wooden box-blinds called "coops," or freestanding camouflage tent-blinds. Both have shooting ports and can be equipped with such amenities as easy chairs and gas stoves.

LADDER STANDS are easy to climb; most are about 12 feet tall. Attach the platform and ladder to the tree with straps or chains.

TRIPOD STANDS, up to 12 feet tall, are ideal in marshlands or brush-lands without large trees. Hide them in the tallest cover available.

CROTCH BOARDS are notched at each end. Wedged tightly into a tree crotch, they provide a comfortable place to sit or stand.

STOP next to cover that breaks up your outline. Keep your movement to a minimum when glassing for deer.

While you're looking ahead, a deer may slip in close and will spook if you move too suddenly.

Still-Hunting

To become a successful still-hunter, you must learn to beat whitetails at their own game. First, you'll have to familiarize yourself with the cover and terrain. Then, you must sneak quietly and slowly along rub or scrape lines, through feeding and bedding areas or along the edge of heavy cover. Stop often and remain motionless for long periods to look and listen for deer. Because of the skill and patience still-hunting requires, many consider it the most demanding, exciting and rewarding deer-hunting method.

Still-hunting is a good technique whenever hunting pressure is light. When hunting activity keeps deer on the move, you'll have better success in a stand. If you're exploring new territory, still-hunting familiarizes you with the terrain and helps you locate good stand sites for future hunts.

Always still-hunt directly into the wind or crosswind, never straight downwind. Whenever possible, hunt with the sun at your back to make it harder for deer to see you, and to keep the sun out of your eyes.

Sneaking silently is the key to successful still-hunting. Damp ground or fluffy snow quiets your footsteps; windy weather obscures any sounds you may make. Don't attempt to still-hunt on quiet days when the ground is dry.

Before you start, remove your rifle sling so it can't hang up on brush and make noise. As you move, watch the ground ahead of you and avoid stepping on sticks or crunchy leaves. Take short steps to keep your balance. With each step, put your weight down slowly; if you feel a twig underfoot, reposition your foot before the twig snaps. Avoid any sudden movements, like swinging your arms or quickly turning your head.

Don't panic if you snap a stick. Freeze and remain motionless. A deer trying to determine the source of a sound may remain alert for several minutes, flicking its tail. Satisfied that no danger exists, it usually returns to what it was doing, and may even move closer to investigate the sound.

Plan each "leg" of your hunt so you can stay near cover, and avoid walking over noisy ground such as loose rocks or crusted snow, or climbing over obstructions such as fallen trees. You may have to crawl under low branches.

Move slowly – no more than a couple hundred yards an hour. Take only a few steps between stops in heavy cover; move farther in mature timber or other open cover.

If you surprise a deer you don't wish to shoot, or if a deer runs away before you can get off a shot, stop moving for about 20 minutes to give it a chance to settle down. If you continue to push the deer, it will spook other deer in its path.

You may be able to stop a bounding deer long enough for a shot by blowing sharply on a whistle.

Experienced still-hunters spend more time standing still than moving. After completing a leg of your hunt, stop next to a tree or deadfall (preferably one in deep shadow), that conceals you and provides a stable rest for your gun. Spend several minutes looking for deer.

As you look, minimize motion by scanning with your eyes without moving your head. If you don't see or hear deer, slowly turn your head to scan 360 degrees. In heavy cover, slowly crouch down to peek beneath branches. Always be ready to shoot, regardless of your position.

After scanning the area, use binoculars to systematically search for ear movements, tail flicks, or shapes and colors you couldn't see with the naked eye. Look for any horizontal line; it could be the back or belly of a whitetail.

Learning to still-hunt takes time. On your first few hunts, you'll probably see more flags in the distance than deer within shooting range. If you're having problems getting a shot, slow down, stop longer, look more and move less. Above all, hone your skills at every opportunity.

How to Still-Hunt in Various Types of Terrain

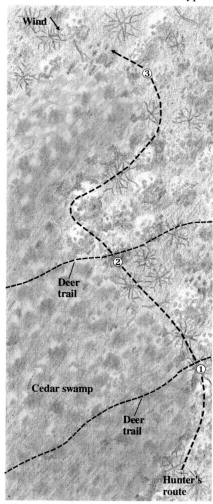

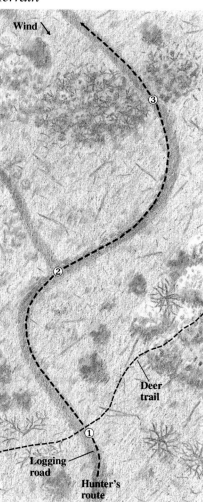

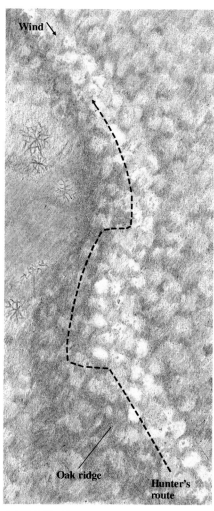

CEDAR SWAMP (or other heavy cover). Hug the outside edge, stopping often to look and listen. Stop longer near (1 and 2) deer trails or (3) points jutting into open timber.

LOGGING ROAD. Stop and watch wherever (1) a deer trail crosses the logging road, (2) another logging road intersects and (3) anywhere the logging road cuts through heavy cover.

OAK RIDGE. Still-hunt a ridge in a zigzag pattern by alternately moving 100 yards along one side, then sneaking across and moving 100 yards along the other side.

OPEN FORESTS. If the terrain is flat, still-hunting is difficult because deer can easily spot your movements from a distance. Take advantage of all available cover, glass often and move very slowly between stops.

Tips for Still-Hunting

PEEK over a ridge inches at a time (left), staying near trees or brush and studying new territory as it comes into view. Never walk over a ridge in an upright position with no cover to hide you (right).

SCAN the cover very carefully, using your binoculars. With the naked eye, a deer at a distance in heavy cover (left) would be difficult to see, particularly in dim light.

Binoculars "open up" the cover, gathering light and helping you spot deer parts (right) that would otherwise be impossible to see.

WEAR outer garments made of quiet, soft-finished fabrics such as wool, cotton or fleece. Wear soft-soled boots so you can feel twigs underfoot.

TIE a downy feather to your bow limb or gun barrel with a piece of strong thread or dental floss. This way, you can constantly monitor wind direction.

YELP on a turkey call to convince deer that your sounds came from a turkey. Use this tactic only when the turkey season is closed.

THE DRIVE LEADER (right) decides where the drive will start. He selects stands from which the posters can cover the most likely escape routes, and sends them to their stands on the course that is least likely to alert deer. He estimates the time needed for the posters to reach their stands, and tells the drivers how fast to walk and how far apart they should stay. He informs everyone where to meet following the drive, then signals for the drive to begin.

Driving

Years ago, deer hunters often organized massive drives. Upward of two hundred hunters joined forces to cover a mile-wide swath of forest, sometimes killing more than 100 deer. Today's drives are much smaller, but no less effective.

The usual drive consists of a group of walking hunters, or drivers, who push deer downwind or crosswind past waiting hunters, or posters. In some southern states, dogs are used to drive deer (p. 120).

Drives work best in isolated patches of cover where deer must eventually funnel through a narrow passage or run into the open. Ideal sites include woodlots, cornfields and sloughs.

Posters often sit in elevated stands; this way, the drivers can easily see them but the deer can't. A high vantage point also allows posters to quickly spot drivers, fleeing deer and likely escape routes.

Another advantage to elevated stands: they're safer than ground-level stands. Because posters angle their shots toward the ground, there's little chance of hitting the drivers. And the posters are above the driver's line of fire. Still, drivers should never intentionally shoot toward posters; the best policy is to shoot only at deer behind the drive line. All deer-drive participants should wear blaze orange.

Every drive should be supervised by a safety-conscious leader, or drive captain, who is familiar with drive-hunting procedures and the local terrain. He is responsible for making sure the area to be driven is clear of hunters, and that drivers and posters are acquainted with the drive area. A map or aerial photo of the locale can be a big help.

Typically, he assigns more drivers than posters. How far the drivers spread out depends on the density of the cover (p. 91). Too much space causes drivers to lose track of each other and allows deer to remain hidden or double back between drivers. Some drive captains assign "flankers" to catch deer sneaking out the "back door."

Although some drivers believe in making as much noise as possible, you'll move just as many deer and get better shots by making a "quiet drive." Walk slowly; your scent will drift ahead of you, causing deer to move along predictable escape routes. Posters should be ready to shoot as deer slowly move past the stand or pause at the edge of cover. Deer driven into the open are usually running and harder to hit.

Always keep the drive moving as planned, even if you kill or wound a deer. If some hunters drop out, deer slip through gaps in the line.

Carefully mark the location of a downed deer, or the spot where you last saw a wounded deer. After the drive, return to field-dress the deer or follow the blood trail. In some states, however, you must tag the animal immediately.

The leader signals the end of the drive, often with a whistle, and all hunters gather at the previously designated point.

Drive-hunters should be familiar with party-hunting regulations. In states where party hunting is allowed, a hunter can shoot his own deer plus deer for other members of his group. Even where party hunting is legal, the group should decide whether to allow it; many hunters prefer to shoot their own deer.

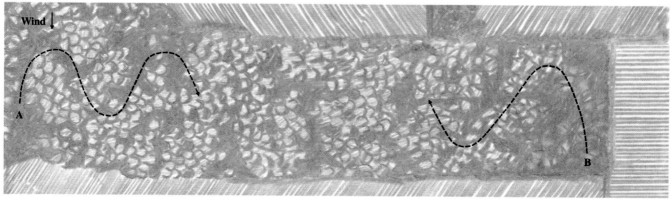

HOPSCOTCH DRIVES are ideal for two hunters. They begin the drive from opposite ends of the cover. Hunter A moves slowly toward hunter B for about half an hour; A then sits quietly for about half an hour as B moves toward him. Because each alternates between driving and posting, both have an equal chance of seeing deer.

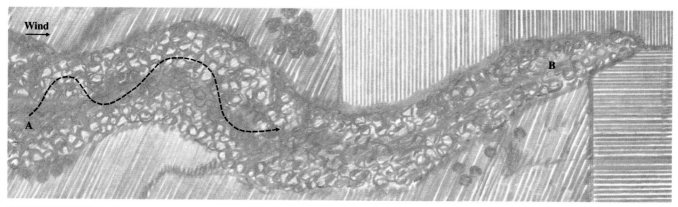

RAVINE DRIVES also work well with two hunters, but wide ravines require more drivers. Select a ravine where the wind is blowing parallel to it and toward its head. Hunter A starts at the bottom of the ravine and begins walking uphill. Hunter B posts near the head, but about 75 yards in from the tip, for shots at slow-moving deer.

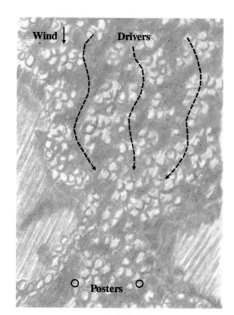

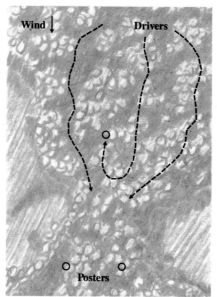

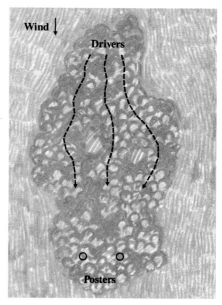

FUNNEL DRIVES take advantage of funnels through which deer are forced by drivers. Funnel drives require fewer posters than drives through wider expanses of cover.

BUTTONHOOK DRIVES prevent deer from slipping back through drivers in heavy cover. As drivers approach a funnel, the one in the center drops out and takes a stand as the drive continues.

ISLAND DRIVES are productive where deer naturally inhabit or have been driven onto islands. Drivers start on the upwind end of the island and walk toward posters on the opposite end.

DRIVERS must stay close enough together to keep deer from doubling back between them. The denser the cover, the closer the drivers should be. In thick cover, the distance may be only 10 yards; in open hardwoods, 100.

POSTERS should hunt from elevated stands, not only for safety, but to better see deer. This hunter has spotted a whitetail and is aiming away from the drivers. Because he's elevated, the bullet is angling downward.

Stalking

Stalking – sneaking to within shooting range of a deer you've spotted – requires sharply honed hunting skills. Many hunters, especially archers, consider slipping up on a whitetail the ultimate hunting challenge.

Open areas, such as agricultural lands, the western plains and large clear-cuts, are ideal locations for stalking because you can see deer from a distance. Stalking is seldom done in forested regions, or where hunting pressure is heavy.

Your chances of stalking deer are best when they're bedded down and the ground is damp enough so you can walk quietly. If the ground is dry, there must be enough wind to obscure any noise you make.

Begin your hunt from a high vantage point and use binoculars or a spotting scope to search the edges of cover for bedded or feeding deer. When you spot one, try to find a landmark to pinpoint the animals location (opposite page).

Stalking Tips

CARRY milkweed pods in your pocket and use the fluff to test the wind as you stalk. If the wind switches, you may have to adjust your route.

Then look for a route that lets you approach from downwind while remaining hidden behind cover or higher ground. Use the landmarks you identified to guide yourself to the deer. It will probably stay bedded in the same location. Slowly and quietly move into position for a shot.

If the deer gets up and is standing or walking slowly as it feeds, move only when it has its head down or is looking away. Keep a low profile and move directly toward the deer; if you stand upright or move sideways, it will probably see you.

If the deer is flicking its tail, it's nervous; don't move until it resumes feeding. However, if the deer begins to move off with its tail or rump hairs erect – and you have a good shot – take it.

Should you get close enough to see the deer but do not have a clear shot, wait patiently until it moves into the open, then shoot.

As you stalk, watch for other deer. If another one detects you, it may snort or flag, warning the deer you're stalking.

Wear soft, quiet clothing and as much camouflage as the law allows, including a face mask (or camo makeup) and gloves. Boots with soft, rubber soles work best. To quietly cover the last crucial yards, remove your boots and stalk in wool socks. Some hunters pull old wool socks over their boots.

Sharpen your stalking skills before the season in parks and refuges with high deer populations or in any areas where you routinely see deer feeding in the open.

GLASS the terrain to find the best route for a stalk. Avoid crossing any openings such as (1) the cornfield in the bottom of the valley, and take advantage of (2) logging roads or deer trails to move as quietly as possible.

MARK the location of a deer (arrow) you've spotted, using a landmark such as a prominent tree or an odd-colored rock. Normally, you'll lose sight of the deer as you stalk, and the landmark will help you find it.

STOP moving if the deer is alert and seems to be focusing all of its attention in your direction. It's nearly impossible to stalk a deer in this situation; wait until it relaxes before proceeding.

FOLLOW a blood trail at night using a bright light. A strong flashlight is best for spotting small drops. Proceed slowly, marking the trail with toilet paper. If you lose the trail, return to the last mark and start over.

Trailing Wounded Deer

Too many hunters buy expensive equipment, travel great distances and spend countless hours hunting, only to lose a trophy buck because they didn't know how to trail it after the shot.

The trailing process starts when you squeeze the trigger or release the arrow. Watch carefully to spot an entrance wound or protruding shaft. Deer hit in a vital area with a single, well-placed shot won't run far and are usually easy to recover. Remembering the details of the shot will help you find a deer that requires trailing.

As you shoot, watch the deer through your sights and study its reactions. A leg, rib or grazing shot usually makes a deer jump and run. A heart or lung shot may produce similar reactions, or the deer may show no immediate response, then bolt away at full speed. But it will seldom go more than 200 yards. A gut-shot deer often holds its tail down and hunches up as it runs. A brain or spinal-column shot will drop a deer in its tracks.

If you miss, the deer may stand still or take a few bounds and then wait to try to pinpoint any further sign or movement, giving you a chance to shoot again. Even if you don't get another shot, follow up your first one. Many a hunter has been surprised to find a dead deer just over the ridge after what he assumed was a sure miss.

If you hit the deer and it runs off, stay put for at least 20 minutes. Many deer are lost because the hunter follows too quickly. Frantic, unplanned pursuits blot out tracks and blood sign that could lead you to the deer. Or they could spook the deer and cause it to run again.

Before trailing the deer, use toilet tissue to mark the location from which you shot. This way, you can easily find it again should you need to backtrack. Walk along the line your bullet or arrow traveled; if you find nicks or gouges in vegetation, your shot may have deflected enough to miss the deer.

Not a promising sign, but follow up anyway

Carefully studying blood at the scene of the shot can provide some valuable clues as to where the deer was hit and how you should proceed in tracking it. Don't disturb the site; mark it in case you need to reexamine it later.

Look for hair around the shot site. Lots of hair most likely means a grazing shot; only a little hair, a body shot. You'll find mostly brown hair if the shot was

This much hair indicates a grazing shot

95

high; white if it was low. Bone fragments, which signify a leg hit, can also be helpful.

The blood trail is your best link to the deer. Always walk beside it, not on it, so you don't destroy clues. If you lose the blood trail, mark the last blood found, then look for overturned leaves, scuff marks or bent plants that may indicate the animal's direction. Deer tend to bleed more when they exert themselves, so you're more likely to pick up the blood trail where a deer has crossed a gully, ditch or fence. If you still

Fresh blood (left) shows up well in artificial light, but dried blood (right) is hard to distinguish from red leaves and grasses

can't pick up the blood trail, systematically search heavy cover nearby. Make every effort to retrieve a wounded animal before resuming the hunt, even if it takes the rest of the day.

Some states allow the use of trailing dogs, which can be a great help in recovering wounded deer.

Despite many claims to the contrary, you can't predict the behavior of wounded deer. They don't always run uphill, or go to water or run a straight course. Do your trailing based on the sign you find, not where you think the deer should go.

Nor can you tell where a deer was hit by the color of the blood. Some maintain that pink blood means a lung hit; dark blood, a liver hit, etc. But even blood experts can tell little about the wound's location based on color.

Don't jump to conclusions based on the first blood sign. The initial blood pattern may be misleading because any wound causes immediate surface bleeding. Look for one of the following patterns to develop:

· Fine droplets sprayed on both sides of the trail for the first 50 to 100 yards. Droplets may be several feet up on tree trunks and brush as well as on the ground. Small bubbles in the blood burst when you touch them. This pattern indicates a hit in the heart, lungs or large blood vessels in the neck.

Fine spray usually means a heart/lung hit

The chances are good that you'll find your deer dead within 200 yards.

· Large splotches of blood at the spot where the animal was hit, turning to continuous drops that diminish within 100 to 200 yards. You may find some clots along the trail. Bleeding continues as long as the deer is moving but stops when the animal lies down. This pattern indicates a hit in the

Big blotches changing to small drops usually mean a muscle hit

leg, back muscles or neck muscles, or rarely, in the body cavity. Eventually, these wounds will stop bleeding, so you'll have to trail the deer based on other clues.

Once you start trailing the deer, move as quickly as possible. If you proceed too slowly, the blood trail will dry and become much less obvious. Always be ready to shoot because you're not likely to find the animal dead.

· Blood trail is difficult to find at first, then large splotches appear between 20 and 50 yards. Blood sign steadily decreases until only scattered specks are found after 100 yards. This pattern is typical of gut-shot deer. Food particles in the area where you

Bits of food or a putrid odor in the blood means a gut shot

hit the deer and putrid-smelling blood confirm a gut shot.

· The volume of blood circulating through the digestive system diminishes as the muscles of a moving deer demand more blood. This, together with clotting, explains why the blood trail thins out after about 50 yards.

· Gut-shot deer are the most difficult to recover. If you suspect a gut shot, wait at least two hours before trailing, even if you fear the deer will spoil or rain will wash away the blood trail. When a deer beds, the blood flow to muscles decreases and flow to the gut increases. The deer will bleed to death in its bed and will be found within 200 to 500 yards, if you don't chase it. But if you follow too soon and spook the deer from its bed, the trail will then have little, if any, blood.

No matter what type of trail you're following, ask your partners for help if you need it. Be sure to tell them exactly what to do. Be quiet, stay together and designate shooters for safety's sake. Someone should stay near the last blood spot and look ahead for the deer while the others search for more blood or tracks.

Always get permission before trailing onto any private land you don't have permission to hunt. Keep track of your location and use a compass – it's easy to get lost when you're concentrating on a blood trail.

Sooner or later you'll come upon the animal. If it's standing or bedded with its head up, shoot it again. Approach a downed deer slowly and quietly from behind, watching for signs of life. If it doesn't move, jab it with a stick. If it does, kill it with a rifle shot in the neck or an arrow in the chest cavity.

Make sure your deer is dead before moving in close

How to Field-Dress Your Deer

When you're certain your deer is dead, tag it, then field-dress it immediately to drain blood and cool the carcass. There's no need to cut its throat. Use a sturdy, sharp knife. A folding lock-back model with a 3- to 5-inch blade is ideal. To field-dress your deer, follow the step-by-step instructions below.

As you field-dress the animal, look for parasites, tumors, growths or spots on internal organs which could indicate a disease. Most of these deer are safe to handle and eat; if in doubt, contact a wildlife professional.

One common and potentially dangerous affliction, however, is Lyme disease, a bacterial ailment that affects humans, dogs and livestock. The first sign of Lyme disease is often a large, reddish rash that forms around the tick bite. But the rash does not appear in all cases. The disease is easily treated in this early stage, but if allowed to advance, it may cause extreme weakness, paralysis and damage to the joints, nervous system and heart.

Some of the ticks attached to whitetails may transmit Lyme disease to humans. In the Midwest and Northeast, the deer tick (also called bear tick, sheep tick or Lyme tick) is the major culprit. In the Southeast, the black-legged tick is the suspected carrier. Recently, researchers have discovered that several other species of ticks and biting insects such as flies and mosquitos can also carry Lyme disease.

How to Field-Dress a Deer (directions for a right-handed hunter)

1. RUN your finger along the breast-bone until you can feel the end of it. Pinch the skin away from the body so you don't puncture the intestines, and then make a shallow cut just long enough to insert the first two fingers of your left hand.

2. FORM a V with your first two fingers, maintaining upward pressure. Guide the blade between your fingers with the cutting edge up; this way, you won't cut into the intestines. Cut through the abdominal wall back to the pelvic area.

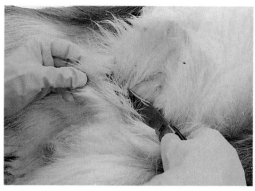

3. SEPARATE the external reproductive organs of a buck from the abdominal wall, but do not cut them off completely. Remove the udder of a doe if she was still nursing. The milk sours rapidly, and could give the meat an unpleasant flavor.

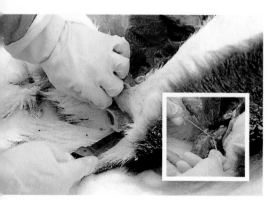

7. CUT around the anus; on a doe, the cut should also include the reproductive opening (above the anus). Free the rectum and urethra by loosening the connective tissue with your knife. Tie off the rectum and urethra with kitchen string (inset).

8. FREE the windpipe and esophagus by cutting the connective tissue; sever them at the jaw. Grasp them firmly and pull down, continuing to cut where necessary, until they're freed to the point where the windpipe branches out into the lungs.

9. HOLD the rib cage open on one side with your left hand. Cut the diaphragm from the rib opening down to the backbone. Stay as close to the rib cage as possible; do not puncture the stomach. Repeat on the other side so the cuts meet over the backbone.

You can reduce the chances of getting a tick bite by treating exposed skin and clothing with a DEET-based insect repellent. But the best protection is permethrin, which is applied to clothing but not exposed skin. It kills ticks that crawl across the fabric.

Wear rubber gloves when you field-dress a deer, and don't cut yourself; infected deer blood in contact with an open wound could transmit the disease.

Don't put the carcass inside a vehicle or near people, pets or livestock; ticks that are not attached drop off soon after a deer dies, and search for a new host. Always check your body and clothing for ticks after a day of hunting.

Ever wonder how the live weight of a deer compares to the dressed weight? As a rule, a live deer would weigh 29 percent more than a dressed carcass.

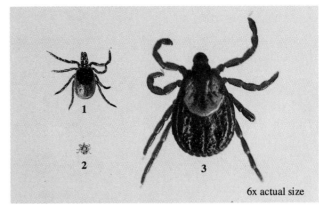

6x actual size

MAJOR CARRIERS of Lyme disease are deer ticks, both (1) female and (2) nymph. Black-legged ticks (not shown) may transmit the disease in the Southeast; they're almost identical to deer ticks. The common (3) dog tick, which is much larger, occasionally carries the disease.

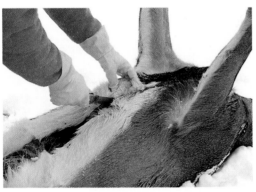

4. STRADDLE the animal, facing its head. Unless you plan to mount the head, cut the skin from the base of the breastbone to the jaw, with the cutting edge of the knife up. If you plan to mount the head (pp. 100-101), skip this step and the next.

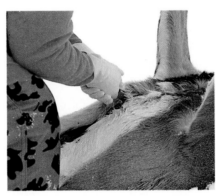

5. BRACE your elbows against your legs, with your left hand supporting your right. Cut through the center of the breastbone, using your knees to provide leverage. If the animal is old or very large, you may need to use a game saw or small axe.

6. SLICE between the hams to free a buck's urethra, or if you elect to split the pelvic bone on either a buck or doe. Make careful cuts around the urethra until it is freed to a point just above the anus. Be careful not to sever the urethra.

10. PULL the tied-off rectum and urethra underneath the pelvic bone and into the body cavity, unless you have split the pelvic bone. If so, this is unnecessary. Roll the animal on its side so the entrails begin to spill out of the body cavity.

11. GRASP the windpipe and esophagus; pull down and away from the body. If the organs do not pull freely away, the diaphragm may still be attached. Scoop from both ends toward the middle to finish rolling out the entrails. Detach the heart and liver.

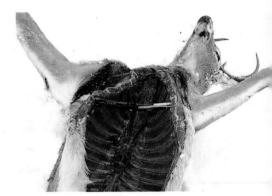

12. PROP the body cavity open with a stick after sponging the cavity clean. If the urinary tract or intestines have been severed, wash the meat with snow or clean water. Hang the carcass from a tree to speed cooling, or drape it over brush or logs with the body cavity down.

Caping Out Your Trophy

If you wish to mount the head of your deer, but have no caping experience, the job is best left to an expert. Though not particularly difficult, caping is time-consuming, and a slip of the knife could mean a less-than-perfect trophy.

Most taxidermists prefer that you bring the entire deer to them, so that they can skin and cape it to their own satisfaction.

If you cannot take the carcass to a taxidermist, the next-best option is to take the entire hide with head attached. To skin the deer, hang it by the hind legs and peel the hide down to the head before severing the neck. From brisket to head, the hide should be free of cuts. The taxidermist can then determine how much of the hide he needs for the mount and do the intricate work of skinning out the head himself.

Should circumstances dictate that you cape the deer yourself, follow the instructions on these pages. Maintain a shaving edge on your knife and work slowly and carefully because any mistake means extra work for the taxidermist.

If you'll be hunting a few more days, hang the cape or hide with head attached in the shade where air can circulate freely. Never place it in any type of container. Trapped air will warm quickly, causing it to spoil. Once home, get it to a taxidermist immediately. If you can't, store it in a deep freeze.

How to Cape Out a Deer

1. MAKE 45-degree cuts (dotted lines) beginning at the inside of the base of each antler. Where the two cuts join, cut straight back along the center of the head to the point where it meets the neck. Make sure your cuts are shallow, through the hide only.

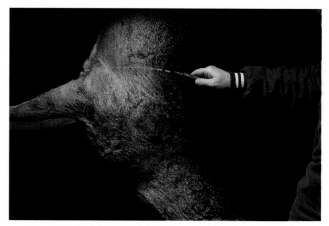

2. START cutting several inches behind the front leg (dotted line) and continue cutting all the way around the body. Make sure you don't angle your cut too far toward the head. If you do, the taxidermist may not have enough hide to work with.

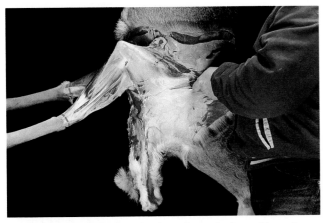

3. CUT around each front leg just above the knee (dotted lines), then cut up the back of the leg to meet the cut around the body. Pull the hide steadily toward the head, freeing any meat or fat that sticks to the hide. Peel down to the base of the skull; sever the head from the neck.

4. PRY the skin away from the antler bases with a screwdriver or other blunt tool. Be sure to get all the hair around the bases. Cut the cartilage that connects the ears to the skull so the ears remain attached to the hide. The taxidermist will finish skinning the ears.

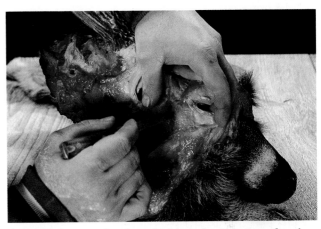

5. SKIN around the eyes with great caution. The skin there, particularly the eyelids, is extremely thin. You could easily cut through it when trying to free it from the skull, especially if your knife is dull. Eyelids are very difficult for a taxidermist to repair.

6. FREE the tear glands at the lower-front corner of each eye. The glands are recessed, so it's important that you cut deep enough and scoop them out. Otherwise, you'll leave a patch of skin on the skull, making extra work for the taxidermist.

7. PRY the mouth open and cut along the gumline to free the upper and lower lips. Pull the cape over the head and, from the inside, cut the remaining tissue at the back of the jaws. Skin the nose from the inside to free the cape; remove any cartilage, fat or meat from the nose and hide.

8. SAW the antlers from the skull by cutting straight down between the antler bases and the eye sockets to a point about 1½ inches below the antler bases. Beginning at the back of the skull, make a second cut (shown) to intersect with the first.

Techniques for Special Situations

See Hunting in Standing Corn (p. 118)

Opening day brings out legions of deer hunters

Tactics for Opening Day

Hunters bag more whitetails during the firearms deer opener than on any other day of the season. Not only are the greatest numbers of hunters afield, but the deer population is at its peak and the opening-day commotion keeps the animals moving. In some states, up to one-half of the annual harvest takes place on the opener.

Stand-hunting accounts for most of the whitetails taken on opening day. Select a good stand and don't leave it until you shoot a deer or legal shooting hours end. Don't check up on your friends, hike to camp for breakfast or walk around to warm up; you'll hurt your own chances but lend a hand to patient hunters who stay put.

In heavily hunted areas, deer have little chance of avoiding opening day hunters. Even novices who haven't taken time to scout and select stands before the hunt have a good chance to score now.

But preseason scouting improves your odds even more. Look for stand sites in the heaviest cover –

Prime Whitetail Funnels

BRUSHY FENCELINES form a funnel between two parcels of wooded cover. A productive fenceline has trees, shrubs or other brushy cover along most of its length.

POINTS of timber jutting into open fields serve as funnels for deer entering the fields to feed and leaving when they're finished.

Daily Deer Harvest and Hunting Pressure Through the Season (figures from Missouri's 1988 nine-day season)

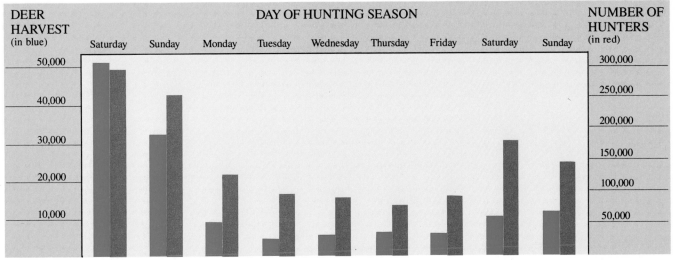

DEER HARVEST (in blue)	DAY OF HUNTING SEASON	NUMBER OF HUNTERS (in red)

DEER HARVEST and number of hunters afield was greatest on the first weekend of the season. On opening day, 297,000 hunters took 51,323 deer for a success rate of 17%. Hunting pressure tapered off during the week, as did harvest and success rate. On Wednesday, 85,000 hunters took 5,267 deer for a success rate of 6%. Hunting pressure and deer harvest increased on the second weekend, but the success rate was the same as during the week.

usually the best bet on opening day. If no heavy cover is available, deer may even bed in the middle of large, open fields, where they are out of shooting range and can see a hunter approaching from a long distance.

If you've hunted the area before and know where hunting pressure is normally heaviest, try to avoid that area on opening day.

As a rule, few hunters venture more than ¼ mile from their vehicles, so it's wise not to hunt within that distance of a road or trail. Mark the access points on a map or aerial photo and highlight the zones to avoid.

Also mark any thick cover beyond the intensely hunted zone. Scout out stand sites in that heavy cover, or on the edge of it. One of the very best stand sites is in a funnel between the cover and the hard-hunted zone (see below).

Despite intense hunting pressure, whitetails attempt to remain within their home ranges. Deer spooked in heavy cover seldom run more than 100 yards; in open country, seldom more than 500.

Cold weather, boredom, stiff joints or leg cramps sometimes make staying on stand difficult. Instead of wandering around, still-hunt to other good stand sites you located during preseason scouting.

NARROW SPITS of land between two lakes form a natural corridor for deer moving between cover and food on opposite ends.

STREAM CORRIDORS form funnels where the timber on either side narrows. The best funnel is where the timber narrows on both sides.

105

Tracking

Tracking combines the excitement of knowing there's a deer just ahead with the suspense of not knowing exactly how far.

Successful tracking usually requires fresh snow; in old snow or dry, fluffy snow, it's difficult to tell the difference between old and new tracks. You may be able to track on damp soil. Tracking works best where there are few hunters to disturb deer, or to shoot the one you're tracking.

A predawn snowfall makes for the best possible tracking conditions. The fresh snow covers up any old tracks, making the new ones easy to follow. And you have all day to locate the deer. Tracking during a light snowfall also works well, but heavy snow fills in the tracks too quickly.

Always wear soft, quiet clothing so you can move silently. Start looking for tracks near rubs, scrapes and feeding areas and along the routes deer travel between feeding and bedding areas. Check established deer trails, edges of standing cornfields, logging roads and power-line corridors.

Once you find fresh tracks, study them to determine in which direc-

How to Determine Age of Tracks in Moist Snow

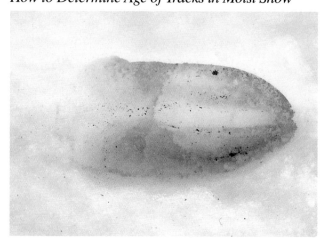

FRESH tracks have sharp edges; snow on the bottom is packed but not frozen.

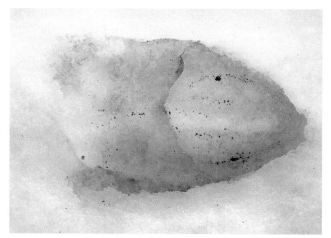

OLDER tracks often enlarge and crumble around the edges as they melt. The bottom may glaze over.

tion the deer are moving, approximate number and size of animals, and their rate of travel.

Follow the tracks cautiously, stopping often to look and listen for deer. If you're too engrossed in studying the tracks, however, a deer may jump up ahead and be out of range before you see it. Move slowly into the wind or crosswind; if you start to sweat, you're going too fast.

Deer often watch their backtrail, so it may be difficult to slip up on them. But if fresh tracks lead toward a bedding area such as a thicket or slough, leave the track, swing wide and approach the cover from the side, keeping the wind in your favor. Watch closely for the bedded deer, but be ready to shoot should it bolt.

Tracks are more subtle and difficult to follow on damp soil, especially when the deer leaves the trail.

Tracks may be tough to follow if the deer leaves the trail

You may be able to follow the deer by looking for overturned leaves or disturbed needles, with moist soil underneath.

Most often, tracking is a one-man operation. However, flankers can intercept deer that jump up ahead and attempt to circle back to stay in familiar cover.

Practice tracking deer after the season closes. This will improve your tracking skills and help you understand the whitetail's habits and travel patterns.

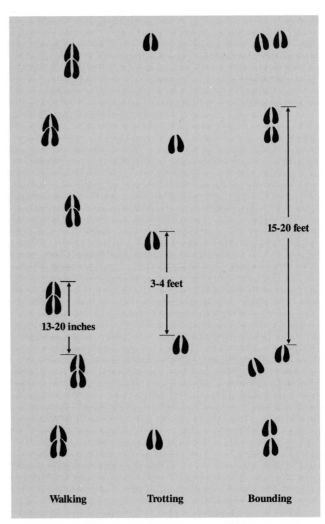

Walking   Trotting   Bounding

GAIT can be determined from track placement. A walking deer (left) places its hind foot almost on top of the track made by the front hoof; the stride is about 18 inches from toe to toe. A trotting deer (center) leaves a line of evenly spaced hoof prints; the stride is about 40 inches. A bounding deer (right) leaves groups of tracks 15 to 20 feet apart, with some bounds measuring more than 20.

How to Determine Age of Tracks in Damp Soil

FRESH tracks have a distinct outer edge and center ridge between the hoof sections. The bottom is damp.

OLDER tracks are not as well defined along the edges and center ridge. The track will be dry if it hasn't rained.

Rattling, Calling & Using Scents

These techniques, intended to attract deer or draw them into range, take advantage of the whitetail's ability to communicate with others of its own kind. None of these will make up for sloppy hunting tactics, but when used correctly, they can greatly improve your odds.

RATTLING. The noise made when you rattle antlers together imitates the sound of an antler battle. Bucks respond to rattling more often than does. Nobody really knows why rattling attracts bucks, but they may be attempting to assert their own dominance, or steal the doe the other bucks are fighting over. Or, they may simply be curious.

Rattling originated in Texas brush country, but is now used almost everywhere. It works best during the rut and for several weeks on either side.

Bucks are most likely to respond to rattling where hunting pressure is light and the buck-to-doe ratio is in balance. Where does greatly outnumber bucks, there is little reason for bucks to fight over does.

RATTLING DEVICES include: (1) real antlers, which produce the most natural sound. Cut off the brow tines and round off the other tines so you don't injure yourself. Run a 3-foot cord through the base of each antler so you can hang them around your neck. (2) Synthetic antlers will do the job if you don't have real ones. (3) Rattling bags, cloth bags filled with hardwood dowels, bring in deer even though they may not sound realistic to humans. (4) Plastic rattling sticks are rubbed together to sound like antlers. One doubles as a grunt call; the other, a doe call.

How to Rattle In a Buck

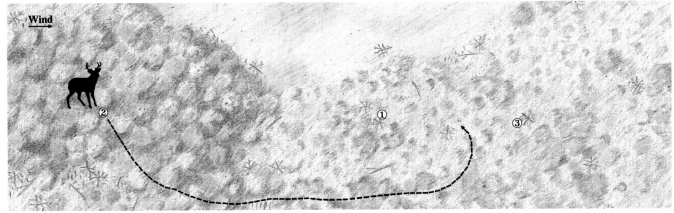

SELECT a (1) rattling site 50 to 100 yards downwind of cover you suspect holds a (2) buck. Start rattling; any buck that responds will probably circle wide (dotted line) and approach the sound from downwind. Consequently, archers often hunt in pairs, with one positioned (3) about 50 yards downwind of the rattler.

Most effective in open country on calm days, rattling does not work as well in heavy timber or on windy days, because sound doesn't carry far enough.

Before rattling, sneak quietly to a stand downwind of heavy cover likely to hold a buck (see diagram). Position yourself so you can easily shoot in a 180-degree zone without shifting.

Begin rattling softly for a minute or two; this way you won't spook any deer nearby. Wait five minutes, watching closely for deer. If none appear, rattle more vigorously for several minutes. Some hunters like to rake brush or paw at the ground with the antlers to simulate the sounds of a fight. If nothing happens, try rattling again or move to another spot. In open country on a calm day, you should move at least one-half mile. In heavy timber or a strong wind, move no more than one-quarter mile.

Always be ready to shoot. When a buck hears the rattling, it usually tries to circle downwind of your position. But it may storm in immediately. Another possibility: it may pause on the edge of heavy cover, or "hang up," reluctant to step into the open. Archers sometimes use a life-size deer decoy or grunt call (p. 110) to draw these hesitant bucks into range.

CALLING. Most calling is done with grunt tubes, which imitate the soft, low-pitch grunts of a buck tending a doe. The sound will attract other bucks and, on occasion, a doe. Calls that mimic the bleat

DEER CALLS include: (1) grunt tube with foot bellows, which frees both hands for shooting; (2) mouth-blown grunt tube, the most common deer call; (3) 2-part friction grunt call, which requires both hands; (4) mouth-blown doe bleat, which allows you to vary the volume and tone and (5) hand-operated doe bleat.

of a doe or mew of a fawn may draw bucks but are more likely to attract does or fawns.

Calling is most commonly done by archers in an attempt to draw deer close enough for a shot. But the technique also helps hunters using shotguns, muzzle-

Calls can draw deer close enough for a good shot

loaders or pistols. Calling may attract deer whether you're on stand or still-hunting.

For best results, call only to deer you can see or hear. Blind calling seldom works; the sound of these calls will travel only about 200 yards under ideal condi-

tions. Call when the deer is standing still. If it's walking, it may not hear the call.

When calling a buck, begin with a short, soft grunt. Often the deer will respond immediately. If it doesn't, grunt once more. If there's still no response, try a series of three short, soft grunts and one longer, slightly louder grunt. If the deer still ignores you, stop calling. Continued calling may do more harm than good.

Once the deer starts in your direction, quit calling; otherwise, it may pinpoint your location and identify you as a threat.

Hunters often make the mistake of calling too often and too loud. Listen to a recording of deer vocalizations to learn what sounds to make. Some hunters can duplicate calls with their own voice.

SCENTS. While nothing can completely disguise human scent, masking scents can confuse a deer long enough for you to get a shot. Common masking scents include bottled fox urine and skunk musk, or

Apply fox urine to a cotton swab and insert under your boot laces

SCENTS used for deer hunting include: masking scents such as (1) fox urine and (2) pine oil, and attractant scents such as (3) buck-urine scent and (4) doe-in-estrus urine-based scent. A (5) dispensing bottle (inset) will slowly drip attractant scent onto a real or mock scrape, making it more appealing to bucks.

Fresh cedar will mask your own scent

natural scents such as fresh cedar leaves. Always use a scent familiar to deer in the area you're hunting. Apply masking scents to your clothing and boots, or to vegetation around your stand.

Attractant scents take advantage of a whitetail's inclination to investigate any urine smell. Doe-in-estrus scent, the most common attractant, is intended to draw bucks, especially during the rut.

Archers sometimes put out scent canisters near their stand. They also make "mock scrapes" by clearing away grass and leaves beneath an overhanging branch and applying doe-in-estrus scent. Dispensing bottles can be used to drip scent into the scrape at any desired rate.

How to Use Attractant Scents

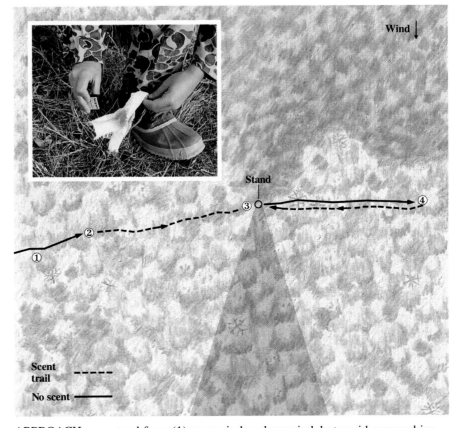

APPROACH your stand from (1) crosswind or downwind, but avoid approaching from anywhere in the shaded area because deer will detect your scent. Tie a drag rag (inset) or attach a scent pad to your boot (2) about 200 yards from your stand to lay a scent trail. When you (3) reach your stand, remove the rag, walk about 200 yards to the opposite side of your stand, replace the rag, then (4) walk back to lay another trail. Freshen the scent about every 100 yards; more often if the ground is wet. A buck that crosses either scent trail may follow it to the stand.

Float-Hunting

Drifting down a meandering stream is an easy way to sneak up on whitetails. They're not likely to hear you coming, and by the time they see you, you're within shooting range.

Float-hunting is a good alternative to still-hunting when the woods are dry and noisy, and it allows you to get away from the crowd.

The technique is legal wherever whitetails are found, but state regulations differ. In some states, for instance, your firearm must be unloaded and in a case when your outboard motor is running.

Most float-hunters prefer canoes. They're light, portable, maneuverable and ideal for shallow water. They easily carry two hunters, gear and a trophy deer. Others feel safer in jon boats or inflatable rafts, which are more stable, but not as maneuverable.

Before attempting to float-hunt, try a preseason float to find launch and take-out sites, learn the stream's characteristics and determine floating time. If the float takes more than a day, locate a good camping area. Along the way, watch for heavily used trails, dense cover and feeding sites, places you will most likely see deer during the season. Talk to landowners before scouting, hunting or camping along the banks.

Ideally, one hunter paddles and steers the boat or canoe from the stern while another in the bow watches for deer and stays ready to shoot. It's important to be quiet and keep movement to a minimum. The shooter should never fire toward the stern.

Float-hunting is difficult on straight, open stretches because deer can easily see you coming. But on a winding stream, you can slip up on them by using the points for concealment.

Before rounding a bend, scan ahead with binoculars to spot distant deer. If it looks like the deer will see you before you float within range, pull your boat up on the bank and stalk on foot.

Waterways can help even if you don't plan to shoot from the craft. You can paddle down a river to silently reach a stand-hunting or still-hunting location. If you shoot a deer close to a stream, you can carry it out by boat.

Always wear a life jacket while float-hunting. Any sudden movement can tip a canoe or small boat, and you could find yourself in icy water. A float coat is warmer than a bulky life vest and doesn't hamper your shooting.

How to Float-Hunt

QUIET noisy watercraft by placing carpet remnants on the bottom and putting pipe wrap over the gunwales. On a canoe, put pipe wrap over the struts, as well.

CARRY a waterproof bag containing a change of clothes, including headgear and footwear; waterproof matches; candles and enough food to see you through an emergency.

HUG inside bends to get within range of deer undetected. As you float (dotted line), (1) stay behind the point. Be ready to shoot as you (2) round the point and can see what's downstream. After rounding the point, (3) cross the stream so you can get a better look at the opposite shore and be in position to round the next point.

Hunting the Suburbs

Suburban zoning ordinances often result in a patchwork of homes, parks and undeveloped land that offers ideal living conditions for whitetails. The combination of excellent habitat and few hunters sometimes results in as many as 100 deer per square mile.

Deer populations this high destroy shrubs, gardens and crops and cause many deer-vehicle accidents. In

Deer-vehicle accidents are common in many suburbs

heavily developed suburbs where deer hunting is not allowed, sharpshooters are sometimes hired to thin the herd.

Outer-tier suburbs, however, usually encourage hunting to help control deer populations. Some hold firearms seasons, but many allow archery only.

When deer become a nuisance, special hunts may be held on nonresidential property such as reserves, parks, cemeteries and commercial land. Inquire at city offices for information on these local hunts.

Stand-hunting is the most practical technique for bagging suburban deer. Even if there were enough space to pursue deer with other techniques, you'd have to get permission from many different landowners.

Locating good stand sites is easy in suburban areas; narrow strips of cover along fences, roads and yards limit whitetails to predictable trails.

When hunting the suburbs, remember that deer may be harder to hear because of background noise such as traffic or airplanes. If you're not watching carefully, a deer could easily sneak past you.

TYPICAL STAND SITES in suburban areas include: (1) the intersection of two tree lines, (2) the corner of a field, (3) a fenceline connecting woodlots and (4) a narrow strip of trees between a pond and an open field. As a rule, the farther your stand from any development, the better your chances for a big buck.

It pays to start lining up hunting spots well before the season begins. Line up as much land as possible to increase your hunting options. Concentrate on large landholdings where you won't have to contact many owners.

Even if you plan to hunt the same spot as last year, get permission early. If the property has changed hands, the new landowner may not let you hunt, so you'll need additional time to find a new spot.

Most suburban landowners have had experiences with "slob" hunters, and are concerned about safety. If you have a hunter-education or firearms-safety card, display it when asking permission.

Should you get permission, determine how many hunters are welcome and provide a list of names. Many owners prefer to deal with only one hunter. Leave your telephone number, describe your hunting vehicle (including its license number), and ask where you should park. Find out if there are times when you shouldn't hunt. Assure the landowner that you will not build a permanent stand. Remove all portable stands when the season closes.

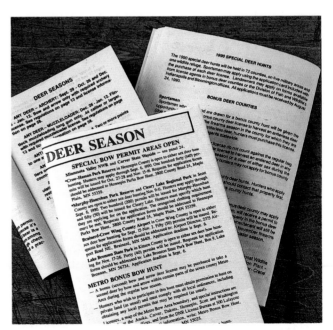

REGULATION BOOKLETS usually list special hunts intended to control deer populations in suburban areas. Read the regulations carefully; in some cases, you may need to apply early for a hunting permit.

Hunting Wetlands

The water and thick cover found in cattail marshes, river backwaters, peat bogs and wooded swamps deter most hunters, but make an ideal hiding place for whitetails.

Deer find wetlands most attractive when other cover is gone – after trees lose their leaves, farmers harvest their crops or snow makes deer conspicuous in lighter cover. Whitetails also move into wetlands to escape the heat.

Although wetlands may offer some food, deer do most of their feeding in adjacent fields and wood-lands around dusk or dawn and at night. During the day, they bed down on high ground within the wetland.

You can stand-hunt along the edge of a wetland in morning and evening. Place a stand, such as a port-able tree stand, along an obvious deer trail between feeding and bedding areas.

But this technique may not work when hunting pressure forces deer to feed mainly at night. In this case, set up a stand within the wetland, overlooking several trails. If there are no trees large enough for a portable tree stand, brace a ladder stand against scrub trees or use a tripod stand. Listen carefully; deer make a lot of noise moving through the heavy cover, so you'll hear them long before you see them.

Jump-shooting may also pay off. Because deer feel secure in the heavy cover, they often hold tight and allow you to get within a few yards before they bolt. Stop frequently to unnerve the deer. Otherwise, you may walk right past them.

Always stay on well-used deer trails when jump-shooting. Keep the wind in your favor and wear hip boots. Confine your hunting to shallow wetlands or those with ice thick enough to walk on.

USE a tripod stand to get high enough to spot deer in a wetland. Most tripod stands have walls to conceal you and are far enough above the ground that deer won't detect your scent.

LOOK for high ground, such as a hummock or small island. High spots often have trees large enough to support a portable tree stand.

WAIT for a wetland to freeze over; this way, you can walk on the ice rather than slog through the muck. But be sure to test the ice first. There should be at least 4 inches for safe walking.

HUNT in wetlands where the cattails have been blown over by wind or bent over by snow and ice. The short vegetation allows you see farther and get a better shot, yet it still provides good bedding cover.

Hunting in Standing Corn

Peeking down a row of standing corn and spotting a whitetail will give any hunter a rush of adrenalin. Cornfield hunters commonly get within a few yards of deer.

Whitetails feed and bed in the corn from summer through harvest time. Standing corn makes good deer cover and offers excellent hunting once the season opens, especially as the harvest progresses and fewer cornfields are left unpicked.

Corn-hunting is most popular with archers, but gun hunters can also use this method, assuming some corn is still standing when the gun season opens.

Before scouting or hunting a cornfield on private land, be sure to get permission. Assure the landowner you won't knock down standing corn as you hunt.

Prior to harvest, look for cornfields that abut woods, thickets, wetlands, ravines and treelines. Isolated cornfields attract fewer deer. After most of the corn has been harvested, look for any corn left standing, such as public or private food plots.

To be sure deer are using a cornfield, scout in and around the field, looking for tracks, trails, droppings and feeding sign. You're most likely to find deer in corn during midday.

Still-hunting is the best method for working standing corn. It's most effective after a hard freeze, when the corn dries and leaves droop, making it easier to see down the rows. Hunting corn is more difficult when the leaves are still green.

It's best to hunt cornfields in windy weather, when rustling leaves mask your sounds. Rain and snow also quiet the leaves. Archers usually wear white, gray or snow-camo clothing, whether or not there's snow on the ground.

Whitetails may be difficult to spot in standing corn. Rarely will you see the entire deer; it pays to use binoculars and look for parts. Remember that whitetails usually bed with their body parallel to the rows.

Another way to hunt standing corn is by driving, but the technique may be dangerous because posters and drivers are on the same level. Drivers should never shoot, and posters must wait until the deer are not in line with the drivers.

If you prefer to stand-hunt, simply wait alongside a well-used deer trail where it enters standing corn. Sit on a 5-gallon bucket or folding stool a few rows from the trail.

How to Hunt Standing Corn

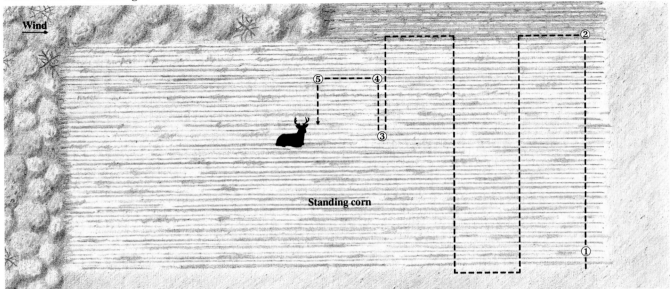

SELECT a field where the wind is blowing parallel to, rather than across, the rows. Begin hunting by (1) walking across the rows on the field's downwind end. Move crosswind, poking your head into each row, looking both ways for deer. When you reach the other side of the field, (2) move up the edge about 60 paces and cut across the rows again. Continue this process until you spot a deer. If it's within range, shoot right away. If not, (3) back up 10 to 15 rows, (4) cut over the estimated distance, then (5) sneak toward it until you have a clear shot. Watch for other deer as you stalk; spooking them will alert the deer you're pursuing and spoil the hunt.

Tips for Hunting Cornfields

LOOK for damaged corn to find where deer have been feeding. You'll see partially eaten ears on the stalks or on the ground.

GRASSY OR BRUSHY AREAS in an otherwise clean field make good bedding sites. Look for wet spots, waterways, or places where the planter plugged up.

"DIRTY," or weedy, cornfields attract more deer than clean ones. Deer feel more secure in the heavier cover, but you won't be able to see as far.

Members of the Bald Mountain Club,

Hunting with Dogs

English and Scottish horsemen used hounds to pursue red deer, or "stags," as early as the 11th century. Settlers from those countries brought this form of deer hunting to the Carolinas and Virginia, and it has since been legalized in more than a dozen southern states. A few other states allow the use of dogs only to recover wounded deer.

Ordinarily, the dogs are used to drive deer to posters. The posters take stands where they expect deer to cross roads, trails or openings. Then other hunters release the dogs. The number of hunters and dogs involved in a drive can number from a few to dozens.

The more dogs and hunters, the larger the block of cover that can be driven. The dogs must be released on the downwind side of the cover because deer tend to flee into the wind. The drive site should not have been "dogged" in the past few days.

Any good hound can find deer and stay on their trail, unless the weather is extremely dry or the deer lose them by running through water. Some hunters favor beagles because they move slowly and don't panic the deer. Consequently, posters get good shots at slow-moving animals. Others prefer larger hounds such as

Walkers, which can cover more ground but push deer harder, sometimes resulting in difficult shots.

When the hounds hit fresh deer scent, they "open up" with a chorus of yelps, bawls, yowls and barks, signaling the hunters to get ready. The "music" means the chase is on and adds to the excitement of the hunt.

If a deer is shot, or the deer being chased are identified as nonshootable, drivers physically catch the dogs or blow a dog horn to pull them off the trail.

Where legal, many hunters prefer buckshot, usually 00 or 000, for close-range shooting at moving deer in heavy cover. In open areas, most hunters use rifles.

Dog hunting is a controversial topic. Many consider it unethical, and some say that deer shot after being run by dogs are unpalatable. If you hunt with dogs, always consider the rights of landowners and other hunters nearby. If your dogs cross land on which you don't have permission to hunt, they may ruin the day for other hunters.

The popularity of dog hunting has diminished in recent years. The method requires a good-sized parcel of land, and if there are several landowners, not all of them may wish to grant permission. Another drawback: keeping a pack of dogs is expensive and time-consuming.

Old Forge, New York, with the results of a dog hunt – circa 1895

VOICES of hounds are distinctive. An experienced handler recognizes the voice of an individual dog and can tell how close it is to the deer by the intensity of its baying.

How to Hunt with Dogs

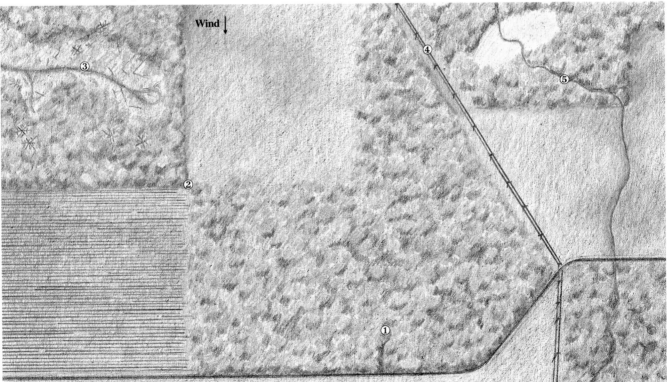

RELEASE dogs (1) on the downwind end of the cover, and post hunters along all natural escape routes. Select stand sites where posters can get clear shots at deer as they (2) cut the corner of a field or cross an opening, such as a (3) logging road, (4) power-line corridor or (5) shallow creek.

Trophy Hunting

What constitutes a trophy depends on what region you're hunting. In the Midwest, for instance, it takes a big 10-pointer to make much of an impression. But in parts of the Northeast, any branch-antlered buck is a trophy.

True record-book racks are extremely rare. Even if a buck has the proper genetics and a nutritious diet, its chances of living long enough to produce a massive rack are slim. What's more, any buck that does live long enough to grow a trophy rack has become adept at eluding hunters.

Hunters who specialize in trophy bucks spend a lot of time determining where to go, scouting for big deer and studying the habits of individual animals.

You could shoot a deer with a trophy rack almost anywhere, but certain "big buck" areas offer the best combination of genetics and nutrition. Remember – heavily hunted areas produce few trophies. The Boone and Crockett Club and Pope and Young Club (archery only) record books can show you where huge whitetails have historically been taken. Many states have deer-hunting organizations that can also provide big buck information.

If you're interested in trophy hunting, tune in on any clues that could help you locate a huge buck. When

Tips for Bagging Trophy Bucks

RUBS on trees at least 3 inches in diameter (left) are usually made by big bucks. Smaller bucks tend to rub smaller trees (right).

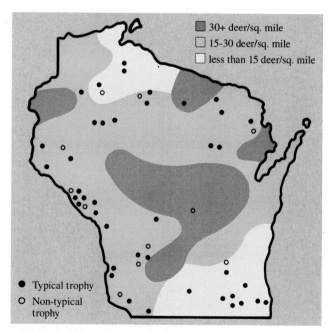

REFER to *Where to Find Whitetails*, published by The Hunting and Fishing Library, for information on trophy hunting areas. This map, part of the publication, shows where trophies have recently been taken by Wisconsin gun and bow hunters. Note that most trophies came from areas with relatively low deer populations.

← *This 461-pound buck, shot in 1955, is the largest ever taken in Maine*

talking to bird hunters, for instance, quiz them on any big-buck sightings and get details on the precise location where the deer was spotted. Or, talk to anyone who spends a lot of time in trophy buck country, like the rural mailman.

If you don't have a specific tip, select a hunting area with large blocks of cover or rough terrain that would make it hard for the average hunter to bag a deer. Begin scouting in early spring. Look for large cast antlers, proof that a big buck survived the last hunting season.

Spend some late summer mornings and evenings near whitetail feeding areas, looking from a distance for big bucks. Hunt the same general area when the season opens. In the early stages of the prerut, place stands where rubs are most numerous; as the rut approaches, along scrape lines; and during the rut, when bucks are chasing does, in high-traffic funnel areas near scrapes.

Because rutting bucks are preoccupied with breeding, they often drop their guard and remain active all day, particularly when hunting pressure is light.

Few hunters have the patience to pursue only trophy bucks. If you're intent on bagging a real trophy, you may have to pass up shots at smaller bucks. Even those who can restrain themselves early in the season have a hard time holding off on a nice buck when the season is winding down.

How to Score a Typical Rack

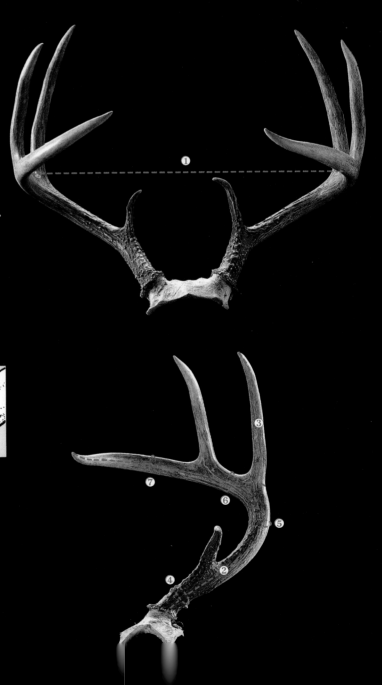

If you think you have a rack that qualifies for the Boone and Crockett or Pope and Young record book, contact the club office or an official scorer for instructions on how to proceed.

Scoring procedures of both clubs are identical. Racks are divided into two groups: typical and non-typical. Minimum scores for typical racks are 170 for Boone and Crockett, and 125 for Pope and Young. Minimum non-typical scores are 195 for Boone and Crockett, 150 for Pope and Young.

Final scoring must be done by an official scorer after a minimum 60-day drying period. However, you can rough-score the rack yourself by taking the following measurements (to the nearest 1/8 inch) with a steel tape.

ADD:

1. Inside spread of main beams.[1]

2. Length of each main beam.

3. Length of all normal points.[2]

4. Circumference at smallest place between burr and first point.

5. Circumference at smallest place between first and second point.

6. Circumference at smallest place between second and third point.

7. Circumference at smallest place between third and fourth point or halfway between third point and beam tip if fourth point is missing.

[1] *Measurement you enter may equal but not exceed the length of the longest main beam.*

[2] *To be counted, a point must be at least 1 inch long, and its length must exceed the width of its base (see illustration).*

SUBTRACT:

A. Difference between inside spread of main beams and length of longest beam, if inside spread is greater.

B. Total length of all abnormal points on each antler.[3]

C. Total of differences between lengths of all points on left and right beams.

D. Total of differences in all circumference measurements between left and right beams.

E. Difference in lengths of right and left beams.

Subtract the total of A-E from the total of 1-7 to obtain the net score for a typical rack.

[3] *Abnormal points are those that originate from other points or from the sides or bottom of the main beam, or extra points beyond the normal pattern of up to 8 normal points, including the beam tip, per antler. To calculate a non-typical score, add instead of subtract the total length of all abnormal points.*

Whitetail Myths

The sport of whitetail hunting abounds with misconceptions, many of which have been passed down through the generations. Though science will never unlock all the whitetail's secrets, decades of research now make it easier to separate fact from fiction.

Here are some of the most common myths, along with the dispelling facts:

MYTH: Trophy bucks are the most elusive deer.

FACT: Trophy bucks are no more elusive than does of the same age. They're seldom seen because there aren't many of them. Antlerless deer usually outnumber antlered bucks at least 2 to 1. Where the buck harvest is heavy, the ratio may drop to 20 to 1, and only about 5 percent of these have a stand-out rack.

MYTH: Bucks are warier than does, often following them at a distance to avoid danger.

FACT: Bucks follow does to determine if they're in estrus, not to avoid danger. When bucks are preoccupied with breeding, they're actually much less wary than does.

MYTH: Bucks often fight fierce antler battles to defend their territory.

FACT: Bucks rarely fight antler battles. When they do, a buck is probably defending a doe in estrus, not its territory.

MYTH: Spooked deer run for miles.

FACT: Deer seldom run more than a few hundred yards and are difficult to push out of their home range. Without familiar cover, they're extremely vulnerable to hunters. Those that do leave their home range usually don't live long enough to return.

MYTH: Wily old bucks often elude hunters for years.

FACT: You may see a big buck in the same vicinity year after year, but it's probably not the same animal because bucks seldom live more than 3½ years. Different bucks may look the same, however, because of inherited antler characteristics.

MYTH: The rut lasts only a few days.

FACT: Actually, the rut may last longer than two months. An individual doe is in estrus for only 24 to 36 hours. However, the estrus cycle of somes does begins much earlier than that of others, and does that are not bred may come into estrus again 28 days later (p. 30).

MYTH: You can tell a deer's age by the size of its antlers.

FACT: Antlers tell you very little about a deer's age because their size is largely controlled by physical condition and genetics. Yearling farmland whitetails, for instance, may be spikes or 8-pointers. The most accurate way to age a deer is to count the growth rings on its teeth (p. 20).

MYTH: If the abdomen is swollen when you recover the deer, the meat shouldn't be eaten.

FACT: When a deer dies, gas from digestion is trapped in the rumen and the abdomen starts swelling almost immediately. However, the meat is still edible. Cool fall temperatures refrigerate the meat and may keep it from spoiling for several days.

MYTH: Rattling only works in Texas.

FACT: Rattling antlers to imitate the sound of bucks sparring may attract whitetails anywhere because bucks always compete for does. However, rattling tends to work better in open areas because the sound travels farther.

MYTH: Cutting the throat on a wounded deer is the best way to kill it and bleed it out.

FACT: Slicing the throat is an inhumane method of killing a deer and doesn't bleed it out any faster than gutting it (pp. 98-99). If the wound does not appear to be fatal, shoot the deer in the head before attempting to field-dress it.

MYTH: It makes no sense to stay on your stand during midday.

FACT: The truth is, hunters who can patiently sit through the middle of the day dramatically increase their odds of killing a deer, especially in heavily hunted areas. Many hunters move around at midday, and their activity moves deer. During the rut, bucks are on the move all day in search of does.

MYTH: When hunting in brushy cover, it pays to use "brush busters," slow, heavy, round or flat-nosed bullets like those used in the .30-30 Winchester, .35 Remington and .444 Marlin.

FACT: Tests have shown that high-velocity, pointed bullets for calibers like the .270 Winchester and .30-06 Springfield are <u>slightly</u> better at penetrating brush than the slower bullets. However, neither type really busts brush; even small branches may deflect them.

MYTH: Doe-in-heat scents should only be used when does are actually in estrus.

FACT: A whitetail buck is ready, willing and able to breed from the time he sheds the velvet from his antlers in early fall until he drops the antlers in winter. Using a sex scent anytime during the hunting season may help attract bucks.

MYTH: You can tell buck tracks from doe tracks because a buck drags his feet more.

FACT: There's no way to determine if tracks were made by a buck or a doe. Either may leave drag marks. However, if the tracks are noticeably larger than other tracks in the area, chances are they're from a buck.

MYTH: If you see small fawns during the hunting season, the deer herd is in poor shape.

FACT: The reverse is true. In years when food is plentiful and weather conditions mild, many of the fawn females become pregnant, but they don't give birth until July, a month or two later than adult does normally would.

When the hunting season opens, these late-born fawns are quite small compared to the fawns of adult does. In poor years, fawn females do not become pregnant, so there are no small fawns when the hunting season opens.

Index

Cy DeCosse Incorporated offers
Hunting & Fishing Products at
special subscriber discounts.
For information write:

Hunting & Fishing Products
5900 Green Oak Drive
Minnetonka, MN 55343